The Homeward Wolf

THE HOMEWARD WOLF

Kevin Van Tighem

RMB

Rocky Mountain Books
www.rmbooks.com

Library and Archives Canada Cataloguing in Publication

Van Tighem, Kevin, 1952-, author
    The homeward wolf / Kevin Van Tighem.

(RMB manifesto series)
Includes bibliographical references.
Issued in print and electronic formats.
ISBN 978-1-927330-83-8 (bound).— ISBN 978-1-927330-84-5 (html).—
ISBN 978-1-927330-85-2 (pdf)

    1. Wolves—Canada, Western. 2. Wolves—West (U.S.). 3. Wolves—Control—Canada, Western—History. 4. Wolves—Control—West (U.S.)—History. 5. Human-wolf encounters—Canada, Western. 6. Human-wolf encounters—West (U.S.). I. Title. II. Series: RMB manifesto series

QL737.C22V35 2013   599.77309712   C2013-903121-9
                                                 C2013-903122-7

Printed in Canada

Rocky Mountain Books acknowledges the financial support for its publishing program from the Government of Canada through the Canada Book Fund (CBF) and the Canada Council for the Arts, and from the province of British Columbia through the British Columbia Arts Council and the Book Publishing Tax Credit.

 Canadian Heritage Patrimoine canadien   Canada Council for the Arts Conseil des Arts du Canada

 BRITISH COLUMBIA ARTS COUNCIL
Supported by the Province of British Columbia

The interior pages of this book have been produced on 100% post-consumer recycled paper, processed chlorine free and printed with vegetable-based dyes.

 MIX Paper from responsible sources FSC® C018246

Contents

Acknowledgements VII

An Absence of Wolves 1

Wolf Journeys 17

Too Many Wolves 43

Not Enough Wolves 61

Cattle Country Wolves 83

The Next, Best Place 123

Bookshelf 143

Acknowledgements

To all the wolf researchers, wildlife managers and wolves who have collaborated over the years (albeit, the researchers and managers more willingly than the wolves) to make this book possible: thank you. And thanks also to the many fine people with whom I've had the great fortune to explore, debate and imagine wolf country, many of whom were kind enough to grant interviews that kept mine from being the only voice here.

Dr. Shelley Alexander reviewed the manuscript in its draft state and offered important criticism. Harvey Locke, Richard Quinlan, Darrell Rowledge and Jesse Whittington were also kind enough to review parts of the text for factual accuracy. Any errors of fact that survived those reviews are my responsibility alone. The opinions are too.

This book is dedicated to the memory of Salix and her pack.

An Absence of Wolves

Western Canada has been wolf country since it melted out from beneath glacier ice fifteen thousand years ago. But growing up in the Calgary, Alberta, of the late twentieth century, I had no idea that my home landscapes were also meant to have wolves.

Real wolves, so far as I knew, lived in the northern forests. To the extent that wolves existed in more familiar places, they lived there in my imagination: vague shadows haunting the edges of the ghost herds of bison that range the misty border between memory and fantasy. They were things of a distant past.

I was amazed, then, when university friends assured me that a few wolves still occupied the most remote parts of the mountains that, on a clear day, we could see arrayed along the western horizon. Could I be, after all, native to a place where the wildest of animals leave snow tracks along frozen rivers and still the night with their eerie howling? The first time I seriously considered it, the thought almost rendered me breathless: the truly wild might not be lost forever after all.

As a student in the early 1970s, I had no car and couldn't afford bus fare. So I started hitchhiking to Banff National Park on the weekends to look for those wolves.

Banff's mountains are not quite timeless, but they're close. In my geology classes I learned that they had been lifted into the sky over a period of forty million years, starting about eighty million years ago. That amount of time is beyond human comprehension, as was much of what my geology professor said, so I didn't bother trying too hard to comprehend it. Instead, I doodled pictures of wolves and spruce trees in the margins of my class notes, and planned my next hike up the Cascade River valley.

Come Saturday morning, I would be chatting with yet another stranger in an unfamiliar car as I watched the Rocky Mountains open their arms and welcome me back to the search for wolves and wildness. They were there somewhere, behind the walls of ancient stone. Sometimes, late in the afternoon, glowing halos framed those peaks. Sunshine gleamed through spumes of spindrift snow streaming across the summits: another birthing chinook.

The wind spilled then, as it does today and has for eons, over the peaks and through the passes into the narrow valleys that drain the Eastern Slopes of the Rocky Mountains. The sound of wind in pines is one of the unchanging things that define that high country. It's the voice of what Wallace Stegner once described as "the geography of hope."

But, at least in the Bow River valley, that wind was different during my young adult years. As it hissed through aging, tooth-scarred aspen stands and grazed-down grasslands, the hundreds of complacent elk whose hair it ruffled fed in peace. No disquieting rumour of hunting wolves drifted down that wind to freeze them in sudden alarm, nostrils flaring. And as their scent eddied through the herds and on into the pines, no wet wolf noses savoured it, with its promise of blood on the snow and warm meat in the belly.

I went to those high valleys looking for wolves

that, in my mind, were the ultimate expression of wildness and ecological wholeness. But I knew I'd likely never find them. Along with virtually all the wolves in southern and western Alberta, the wolves that had ranged the southern foothills and Rocky Mountains had succumbed, two decades earlier, to a government-sponsored killing campaign involving traps, guns and countless poisoned meat baits. Only the first few were now beginning to find their way home from the far refugia that had saved them.

This might still be wolf country after all, but only barely.

And yet ... one day in late April, 1975, as I struggled up the Cascade River valley through the chinook-softened corn snow of an early mountain spring, several sets of hand-sized tracks appeared out of the woods. Six wolves had emerged out of mystery to precede me up the valley. Western Canada's wilderness past and the possibility of future wildness had converged in the here and now.

This was my world transformed, and it was real. Wild wolves had stood in those tracks only a few hours earlier.

Where had they come from? I had no idea. There were more-isolated valleys to the north – the Panther, Red Deer and Clearwater. Was this a pack of wolves that had managed to find security there and only now ventured farther south in search of prey? Their tracks wandered sometimes into the rotting snow beneath the lodgepole pines, then back to the fire road before veering down onto the still-frozen edge of the river. Much of the time it seemed as though I were following only a single animal; each had placed its feet in the same place as they followed their noses into the wind.

At length the tracks turned down through the woods to the river one last time, and I was alone again on the fire road. The hardened edges of week-old bear tracks, peppered with snow fleas, had helped support my weight earlier in the day but by late afternoon the warming snow pack had gone soft. The wet slush was heavy and deep. My boots were sodden. I had hoped to make it all fourteen kilometres to Stoney Creek but, with the evening chill deepening and shadows spreading across the valley, I gave up early. Wet and exhausted, I spread out my tent as a ground sheet on a patch of dry grass at the edge of the timber and threw my sleeping bag on top.

I was asleep before the last light faded from the sky.

It was pitch-dark when I woke at ten-thirty. Every nerve ending in my body vibrated with total, instinctive terror. Two wolves were howling only a few metres away. I had never heard any sound so wild, resonant and intense before. I had certainly never imagined that my first time would find me alone and vulnerable, and the wolves so near.

The last low note echoed off dark, impassive cliffs across the valley. The stars were cold and distant. All was still, except the pulse hammering in my chest. Then, farther up the valley, there came one answering, distant howl.

Silence again, except for the distant murmur of the Cascade River. The night was vast and lonely. Dawn was an eternity away.

I lay awake most of that night, contemplating my own mortality, listening, wondering where the wolves were and what I should do if they were to appear in my little clearing. Huddled down in my sleeping bag, I reflected on the fact that humans are actually remarkably defenceless creatures. My only real defence against a wolf attack was faith in the assurances I'd gotten from reading about them, that wolves had thus far never been known to kill a human in North America.

Fortunately, that defence held: no yellow-eyed shadows appeared. In the morning the tracks showed where two wolves had separated from the rest of the pack to investigate my camp. Farther up the valley, all six tracks reunited. Curiosity satisfied, the wolves were long gone, at least physically. They remained a part of me – no longer imagined but real, in a profound and personal way.

It wasn't long before that particular pack was, in fact, permanently gone. Government trappers, responding to complaints from ranchers along the lower Ghost River a few kilometres away, poisoned six wolves later that spring. Once more, a waiting stillness settled over the Cascade valley. Landscapes are patient. Other wolves would eventually be coming down the homeward trails.

Boom Times in Wolf Country

Not too far downstream, Alberta was booming. In the late 1970s, the aging, agriculture-focused Social Credit dynasty had collapsed. A new Progressive Conservative government full of oilmen and urban professionals, led by Peter

Lougheed, was determined to modernize Alberta and diversify the economy away from its twin mainstays of agriculture and petroleum. They had the money, too. Millions of dollars were rolling into government coffers from the oil patch as world petroleum prices climbed in response to events in the Middle East.

Tourism was among the Alberta government's new investment priorities. Although the mountain national parks consist of federal land that was never ceded to the province, businesses there pay provincial taxes and bring millions of tourism dollars through international airports in Calgary and Edmonton. With more money than it knew what to do with, the new government made sure that some was directed, through grants and loans, to tourism operators in the national parks. Soon, there were virtually no businesses in Banff and Jasper that didn't have expansion plans and access to capital. Parks Canada found itself scrambling to develop the necessary science, policy tools and capacity to protect the parks from Alberta's ambitions and wealth. Meanwhile, the tourism boom threatened to turn the Bow valley, in the heart of the park, into a sprawling commercial playground.

Oil fuelled the tourism boom in wolf country in other ways too. Cheap gas helped double traffic volumes on the Trans-Canada Highway between 1965 and 1980. Originally built with just a single eastbound lane and a single westbound lane, the highway was at the limit of its design capacity. Impatient drivers – especially on big weekends during the ski season – were causing alarming numbers of accidents. Many of those were collisions with animals simply trying to cross the road.

The first wolf recorded in the Bow valley in the 1970s was dead. Wardens found it on the highway.

Outside the federal parks, forestry offered Alberta another option for economic diversification. In the early 1980s, the Alberta government sent some of its oil revenues north to help eight existing or new pulp mills expand their operations in the boreal forest. A pulp mill needs an assured supply of wood fibre, so each of the companies was also granted a long-term forest management agreement giving it the right to log trees from the surrounding landscape. By the late 1980s, forest companies had tied up almost all the forested land outside of parks.

Those companies promptly began building new roads. Those roads brought guns and traps into new corners of wolf country. The spreading patchwork of clearcuts along those roads, however, yielded lush regrowth of shrubs and deciduous trees. Populations of white-tailed deer, elk and moose exploded. It might now be easier for a wolf to die early, but the odds had also improved that it would produce a lot of well-fed offspring first.

One major exception to the clearcutting of Alberta's forested wolf country was south and east of Banff National Park. There, the Lougheed government opted to develop a nature playground they felt would be even better than the expensive federal parks at Banff and Jasper. Kananaskis Country opened in 1977, with newly paved roads through spectacular mountain scenery and a multiple-use mandate tilted toward nature-based tourism and recreation. It also came with a major hotel, golf and ski resort development at the confluence of Evans-Thomas Creek and the Kananaskis River – some of the most productive and important habitat for sheep and elk in Alberta and, until then, a good place for wolves.

The cumulative effect of all these changes was

to fill the eastern slopes of the Rockies and the southern fringes of the boreal forest with new roads, growing towns, more industrial activity and many more people. None of those changes, wildlife research has shown, are good for wary animals like wolves.

But the wolves were coming home anyway.

Pioneer Wolves

By the late 1970s, park wardens knew that wolves were raising pups in a den in the remote Panther River valley of Banff National Park. From there, the pack's travels took them through the adjacent Cascade and Red Deer valleys, sometimes even to the edges of the Bow valley. The rush and clamour of vehicle traffic on the Trans-Canada Highway, the long clatter of passing CP trains and the smell of all those people doubtless helped persuade the wary newcomers to turn around and head back again.

I had been fortunate enough to land a position as a biologist with the Canadian Wildlife Service in 1977. I worked with a team led by Geoff Holroyd on a comprehensive wildlife inventory of Banff and Jasper National Parks. My base was in Jasper, where wolves had managed to hang on through the twentieth century's predator wars. Wolves and I were crossing tracks regularly by the time our study concluded in 1981.

They still hadn't reclaimed the southern Rockies, however. In the final wildlife inventory report we concluded that, in Banff, "wolves are approximately eight times less common than in Jasper ... Wolves are most common in the Front Ranges, particularly the Clearwater, lower Red Deer River, Panther River and middle Cascade River watersheds.... At present, wolves are only sporadic visitors to the Bow valley. There were only two sightings of single wolves, one track and one scat recorded from the Bow valley between 1976 and 1980."

After a century of unpleasant experiences with human beings, it seemed doubtful that any wolves would ever want to share the Bow valley with the more than five million residents, visitors and transients who annually crowd its narrow confines. The Trans-Canada Highway was a wildlife death trap. Warden Hälle Flygare tallied over two hundred large mammals killed annually along the asphalt strip that some of his colleagues had begun describing as a "moving wall of steel." Elsewhere, the town of Banff was expanding from one side of the valley to the other. Roads, campgrounds, picnic areas, gravel pits, an airstrip, outlying bungalow camps, an army cadet training centre and the Canadian Pacific railway occupied more than 10 per cent of the valley floor.

Those of us who suspected in the early 1980s that the Bow valley was just too far gone to support wolves were wrong. When it comes to wolves, it's easy to be wrong. Most of what we think we know about these formidable predators is as much the product of our biases, emotions and attitudes as it is of objective fact. Wolves are what they are, not what we think they are.

When a rancher friend once asked, rhetorically, what the point of wolves was, I jokingly responded that "the wolf was sent to test us." In retrospect, I wonder if that response didn't come close to at least one kind of truth. If so, we have yet to pass that test.

We could, though. The wolves keep coming home. Those who wish they'd stay gone might be inclined to say that it's like wolves aren't getting the point. Another perspective, however, is that we're the ones who haven't yet gotten the point. Eventually, we will.

Wolf Landscapes

Wolves are coursing predators. They wander widely in search of prey. There is a Russian saying: "A wolf is fed by its feet." Especially in winter, when frozen lakes and rivers make long-range travel easy, wolves can travel seventy-five kilometres or more in a day, and then repeat the performance the next day and the next.

Early in the summer, when the pups are young, a wolf pack may limit its travels to an area as small as fifty square kilometres, but once the young ones are mobile, the pack may roam over home ranges from one thousand square kilometres in Alberta to more than five thousand in subarctic tundra habitats. Wolves, by nature, are creatures of the whole landscape. Whatever happens on the landscape – a fire or landslide, a new road, a dam, mine or rural subdivision – is bound to affect the wolves who live there.

That's the physical landscape. More so than almost any other animal, however, the wolf is a creature whose survival depends on its ability to navigate another landscape – an unseen landscape of human imaginings, ambitions, fears and identity. The physical landscape may be ideal for wolves – frozen winter rivers, unroaded forests, broad valleys and abundant deer and elk – and yet, if the unseen landscape of the human mind overlying that geography is hostile to their survival, it will be a place where wolves only go to die. That's been the situation since the late nineteenth century in most of southern Alberta.

On the other hand, the physical landscape may be a maze of complications that confound wolves' daily travels and compromise their ability to hunt, raise pups or disperse, but they will nonetheless persist, or even thrive, if the unseen human landscape is favourable. When I came back to the Bow valley of Banff National Park in the early twenty-first century, that's what I found.

There is no question that Banff's development and tourism history has given its wolves a complicated landscape, full of pitfalls, traps and barriers. But they're okay with that, because people want them alive – at least, in the Banff part of Alberta's human landscape.

Biologists estimate that perhaps five thousand

wolves live in Alberta, if you place much stock in population estimates of mobile, elusive creatures that breed prolifically and die in so many ways. Humans are easier to count: well more than 3.5 million people live here now.

It may once have been possible to speak of the physical landscape and the social landscape as two separate things, although most Aboriginal people would likely dispute that. In any case, it is no longer possible in the crowded West of the twenty-first century. Just as the physical landscapes we occupy shape how we live and think, so do our attitudes, biases, knowledge and ignorance shape and reshape those landscapes. The place shapes the people; the people shape the place. Ultimately, Alberta's seen and unseen landscapes are the same place – wolf country.

In studying to understand the fate and future of the wolves with whom we share these home places, then, we are sure to learn as much, or more, about ourselves.

Wolf Journeys

Jesse Whittington knows the wolves of Banff National Park about as well as anyone can. The soft-spoken Parks Canada biologist has logged thousands of hours tracking wolves and other wide-ranging carnivores throughout the mountains, capturing and fitting them with radio collars and trying to figure out how they live and why they die.

Like other Parks Canada resource conservation specialists, Jesse feels the loss of individual study animals at a personal level. Even so, he works at staying focused on what their fates signify about the health of park ecosystems and the long-term strategic issues facing the wolf population as a whole.

He's been around Banff's wolves long enough to have seen the changes in the national park's wolf society over the past couple decades and to develop some ideas about why things happen the way they do.

Jesse and other wolf experts believe that a few wolves likely survived throughout the latter half of the twentieth century in the remote Red Deer and Clearwater valleys, even during the dark years of the 1960s and early 1970s. But something changed in the 1980s, and the solitary wanderers and ephemeral groups began to cohere into discrete packs. One factor may have been the growing number of elk in the upper Red Deer valley. Increasingly restrictive hunting regulations outside the national park, combined with a series of mild winters, resulted in the estimated number of elk wintering on the grassland ranges of the Ya Ha Tinda Ranch, just east of the national park boundary, growing from only five hundred in the mid-1970s to more than two thousand a decade later.

Around the same time, wolves began denning regularly at their ancestral den locations on the small relict grasslands along the Red Deer. There are historical den sites on the Ya Ha Tinda as well as most of the larger alluvial fans upstream along the river.

Hunting and trapping pressure is high in the part of the Red Deer valley lying outside Banff National Park. As recently as 2012, trappers and hunters killed at least thirteen wolves on the Ya Ha Tinda alone. But with abundant and growing prey herds, wolves that survived each winter's assault were able to produce large litters and raise most of their pups to maturity. The population grew.

The Red Deer pack was one of three packs whose home ranges overlapped on the Ya Ha Tinda Ranch. Some years, the Red Deer pack denned right on the Ya Ha Tinda; other years they denned farther upstream in Banff National Park. The pack's hunting forays took it as far as the Red Deer headwaters and adjoining Pipestone River drainage, just north of Lake Louise.

In the winter of 2008/2009, the Red Deer pack's alpha (breeding) female, known to Jesse and other researchers as Chinook, choked to death in a trapper's snare – a common death for Alberta wolves. The loss of an alpha animal has a destabilizing effect on a wolf pack, sometimes causing it to disintegrate into two or more smaller packs and other times causing it to change its hunting habits or home range. With the death of Chinook, the pack abandoned the Red Deer valley, crossing a drainage divide into the adjoining Pipestone watershed before finally taking up residence in the middle Bow River valley, near Castle Mountain.

They weren't the first wolves in the Bow valley, however. Wolves had finally reclaimed that crowded corner of the Rocky Mountain landscape in 1986. Ecologist Cliff White found the first Bow valley den that year, even as Parks Canada was finally beginning to turn the tide on the development, roadkills and forest ingrowth that had made the valley increasingly inhospitable. When the Red Deer pack arrived in 2008, there were already two other packs living there.

The Fairholme pack denned on the slopes below the Fairholme Range near Lake Minnewanka and hunted the lower Bow valley and nearby Cascade and Ghost valleys. The Bow Valley pack denned near Johnston Canyon and spent most of its time in the middle Bow valley with occasional forays downstream or south across Vermilion Pass into Kootenay National Park.

Soon after the Red Deer wolves arrived and established themselves in the lower Pipestone and

Castle Mountain area, the Bow Valley pack began to deteriorate. Some of its yearlings dispersed, as yearlings often do. Other pack members died on the Trans-Canada Highway, which at that time still had some unfenced portions. But something was wrong with the survivors too. Jesse and other biologists noticed that their coats were in poor shape and they looked unhealthy. Nobody managed to find the cause – they could have come down with mange or some other disease, or have been inadvertently or deliberately poisoned – but in a matter of months the original Bow Valley pack was gone.

The former Red Deer pack didn't take long to shift its centre of activity down-valley to the now-vacant middle Bow valley. A lot more elk, deer and sheep live near Johnston Canyon than in the Lake Louise area. In 2010 the one-time Red Deer pack became the new Bow Valley pack, even moving into one of its predecessor pack's former den sites the following year. The change in venue brought a change in behaviour too, as if the wolves had sensed that people in the Bow valley were more kindly disposed toward them than the armed adversaries they had dodged in the Red Deer. Unlike the shy and elusive Fairholme pack, the new Bow Valleys were soon as unconcerned about people as their predecessors had been. Tourists and photographers could pull to the side of the Bow Valley Parkway and watch the wolves playing in an adjacent meadow or trotting right along the edge of the road on one of their hunting forays.

Researchers, park wildlife staff and professional photographers probably helped make the wolves a bit too comfortable around people. Some notorious local photographers virtually camped on top of the wolf pack, shadowing them through the valley and building illegal blinds close to the den sites, a practice that wolf researchers had previously abandoned as unethical. Parks Canada restricted morning and evening road access to one side of the Bow valley to give the wolves solitude and peace during the critical late winter and spring seasons, but several Canmore-based photographers simply used the restricted periods as opportunities to get even closer to the wolves. Frequently harassed wolves often move away, but these ones, fortunately, simply learned to ignore the paparazzi.

Trusting wolves are a treasure for commercial

photographers and provide hours of richly reward-ing wildlife viewing to national park visitors. The problem, however, is that their trusting natures can get those wolves shot when they wander outside park boundaries. The low-volume, low-speed Bow Valley Parkway also helped the wolves to feel safe walking on asphalt – a habit that proved fatal for some that managed to get onto the nearby Trans-Canada Highway. Parks Canada only finished the gargantuan task of fencing the entire highway in 2012.

Steve Michel, like Jesse Whittington, works with Banff's wolves on a regular basis. As a wildlife–human conflict specialist, however, he is more concerned with the day-to-day management of wolves than with research to understand them better. The Bow Valley pack poses troubling ques-tions for him:

> At one level, I think it's a very unique, incred-ible national park experience. People can drive down the Bow Valley Parkway and see a pack of wild wolves frolicking in the meadow a hundred feet away from their vehicle. They can stop and take photos of them for fifteen

minutes, and it literally changes people's lives. I've had people send me notes about that, and photos, and it is the most remarkable experience they've ever had in their lives. It's the same thing that happens down in Yellowstone, in places like the Lamar valley.

What concerns me is that Banff National Park is still a relatively small place for a wide-ranging animal like a wolf. So when those wolves decide to wander elsewhere, they have this naive idea of what people mean and what vehicles mean and how they should react to them. They don't get to go very far outside a park boundary before they'll have an encounter with a human being that is very different. If they disperse just a couple hours south, outside the corner of Kootenay National Park – literally, it's a couple hours of travel for those wolves to go from the Bow Valley Parkway to just outside the park – [when] the first vehicle pauses on a road that they're standing and looking at, which they've done hundreds of times on the Bow Valley Parkway, [they are] going to be greeted by someone coming out of the truck with a rifle, and that is the end of the story for them. It's the same situation if they disperse to the east in Alberta.

So it becomes one of those discussions about "how should we be managing those wolves?" Should we keep being hands-off, just allowing them to be very tolerant of people and have a very high level of habituation? Or, for the sake of their longevity, should we actually be hazing them or managing them more so they develop a fear of people, so that as they disperse or make forays into different areas, they may be less likely to get shot and killed?

It's a tough one.

Skoki's Journey

Skoki was one of the new Bow Valley pack pups born in 2009. Late that year, Jesse Whittington and his colleagues caught him and fitted him with a radio collar. Biologists wanted to find out how much time the pack spent in nearby alpine areas where Parks Canada was considering reintroducing the recently extirpated woodland caribou. Skoki's collar recorded GPS locations at regular intervals, revealing that the pack not only spent a lot of time in those remote alpine meadows but actually crossed glaciers and hunted and killed mountain goats, animals whose cliff-dwelling habits usually keep them safe from wolves.

Those findings didn't bode well for any future attempts to reintroduce caribou to Banff.

Late in 2010, having reached sexual maturity, Skoki left the pack as a disperser and headed out of the national park. Because he had grown up relaxed around humans and their roads, and now faced a landscape full of both, the odds were not on his side.

Skoki crossed the Trans-Canada Highway safely, funnelled onto one of Parks Canada's new wildlife crossing structures by kilometres of wildlife fencing installed over the previous decade. On the south side of the highway he made it across the CP rail line and approached the town of Banff, which sprawls almost to the foot of Sulphur Mountain. There, he made a fortuitous decision: he turned right.

Parks Canada had halted the town's expansion in the 1990s, leaving a narrow strip of undeveloped forest south of the town, just below the Upper

Hot Springs. The last building in that wildlife corridor – the historic home of Alpine Club of Canada founder A. O. Wheeler – had just been demolished when Skoki made his way through its sheltering pine forests. Steering well clear of the Banff Springs Hotel and its sprawling golf course, Skoki veered right again, out of the narrow wildlife corridor and into the Spray River valley. There, he needed only avoid a few diurnal cross-country skiers to work his way up to the park boundary and out into the Spray Lakes area of Kananaskis Country.

Big-game hunting season was over, so Skoki encountered none of the flying bullets his predecessors had found in BC. And now, in the Spray River headwaters, the landscape made it difficult for him to get back to the Bow valley, where death-by-highway awaited. To get there, he would have had to follow a road and hydropower canal into Whiteman's Gap and then get around the valley-clogging town of Canmore. Instead, he journeyed south down the wide Smith-Dorrien Creek valley to the Kananaskis River.

This was all new country for the young wolf, so he spent some time wandering up side valleys and over high passes into the upper Elbow, Sheep and Kananaskis valleys before returning to the main valley. Wildlife biologist Cam McTavish traced the wolf's route both by following tracks in the snow and downloading GPS locations from the transmitter in Skoki's radio collar. Cam found the remains of more mountain goats; Skoki's unusual hunting specialty had survived the move.

Skoki's timing was ideal: there was no resident wolf pack in the upper Kananaskis, and prey was abundant. Meeting up with one or two other wanderers, the young wolf soon became the alpha male of a new pack that ranged mostly in the head-waters of the Kananaskis River. Another pack appeared farther downstream in the Evans-Thomas area that same winter.

As they had before and will again, wolves had found their way back to the Kananaskis valley.

Blizzard's Journey

Skoki's little sister didn't fare so well.

Originally named wolf 1101 by unsentimental biologists after the number of her radio collar, she was soon renamed "Blizzard" by the local wildlife paparazzi. She too left the new Bow Valley pack as a disperser, a year after Skoki. Approaching the town of Banff, Blizzard turned left where her brother had turned right. She likely worked her way along the elk-rich Vermilion Lakes wetlands until it was too late to get around the town on its south side. Instead of squeezing through the safety of the narrow wildlife corridor at the base of Sulphur Mountain as her brother had done, Blizzard chose a more perilous route along the railway line between the main town and its industrial compound area.

Her radio collar – fitted with a remote-release mechanism preprogrammed to release the collar when the battery pack grew weak – came off there, within a few hundred metres of the Parks Canada warden office. It was almost as if she were returning it to its home base. The rest of her journey went unrecorded by the GPS-based data logger in the collar.

Once Blizzard was safely past the town of Banff, the journey along the Bow River to the national park boundary would have been uneventful. Somehow she made it around or through the town of Canmore, a sprawling conglomeration of condominiums and trophy homes that, since the mid-1980s, has grown to fill much of the Bow valley east of the national park boundary. A recent census found that the town has more dogs than children; doubtless Blizzard's nostrils were under constant assault by their various odours as she picked her way through the narrow alleyways of pine trees that separate the subdivisions of mostly empty weekend homes.

At the east end of Canmore, where Wind Creek's alluvial fan pinches out against the steep forested slopes of Pigeon Mountain, she encountered another stretch of highway fencing similar to what Parks Canada has installed inside the national park. Here, she had to choose whether to stay in the narrow strip of forest on the south side of the highway or to cross under a poorly screened wildlife underpass to the toe of the Wind Creek fan and its adjacent wetlands.

Regardless of which choice she made, Blizzard's options shrank almost to nothing when the fence ended, a kilometre or so farther east.

There, where the cliffs of Pigeon Mountain and Mount MacGillivray squeeze the Trans-Canada Highway right against the riprap-armoured edge of Lac des Arcs, wolf 1101's unfortunate route choice cost the wandering yearling her life.

Just after Christmas 2011, Alberta Parks ecologist Melanie Percy retrieved the young wolf's carcass from the edge of the asphalt – another Bow valley road-kill. In an interview with the *Rocky Mountain Outlook*, Melanie said the death was no surprise: "That is a real pinch point for wildlife movement there. Due to the natural- and human-caused fragmentation, there is limited opportunity for movement."

Canmore has resident cougars and, in season, black and grizzly bears. But it is hostile terrain for a travelling animal like the wolf because of the fractured movement corridor to the east, the network of both official and unauthorized recreational trails along the valley slopes, and the steep mountain walls that block travel north or south. Wolves hoping to travel to or from Banff National Park's productive wildlife ranges have to avoid this patch of dead ground, either by following the Spray or Brewster valleys south or turning north along the Cascade valley or through Devil's Gap to the Ghost River.

It could have been a whole lot worse. In the

1980s, the town of Banff was well on the way to plugging the entire Bow valley inside Banff National Park. The still-unfenced Trans-Canada Highway, meanwhile, was killing dozens of animals every year. The Banff–Bow Valley Study of the early 1990s – an exhaustive analysis of ecological conditions in Banff that the Canadian government had commissioned in response to public concern about out-of-control tourism development – confirmed that development was on the verge of ruining Canada's first national park.

In response, Parks Canada put a fixed boundary and a permanent growth cap on the town and began to remove outlying developments to create narrow wildlife habitat corridors north and south of the town. Over the following fifteen years it also spent over $100 million to enclose the highway with tall wildlife-proof fences, while building eight massive overpasses and more than forty underpasses to ensure that wolves and other animals could again safely cross the "moving wall of steel."

While urban sprawl was turning the Canmore corridor, further east, into dead ground for wolves, Parks Canada was working hard to make the rest of the Bow valley habitable again. They succeeded.

The wolf packs that have returned to their ancestral den sites in the Bow valley, in spite of Geoff's and my doubts a few years earlier, will continue to send dispersing youngsters into the surrounding landscape. With any luck, most will continue to avoid the death trap east of Canmore and, instead, traverse Banff's painstakingly restored wildlife corridors and connecting wilderness valleys to find new homes in the mountains and foothills farther north or south.

Wolves by Airmail

There are other ways for wolves to get around that have nothing to do with the wiring of their genes or, for that matter, the health of the landscape. They can travel by airplane, for example. It's stressful but it works very well.

Poison, traps and guns were even more effective south of the forty-ninth parallel than they were on the Canadian side during the twentieth century. Ranchers and government waged as relentless a war against large predators as against the original Indian nations of the west. Even the national parks got into the act. Yellowstone was hard at work poisoning off its wolves by 1877, five years after it was established as the first national park in the world. The last Yellowstone wolf was killed in 1926. By the 1950s, no wolves survived anywhere in the western United States, and only a few dozen were hanging on in the northern corners of Michigan and Minnesota.

Elk populations, predictably, exploded – especially in the national parks, where human hunting wasn't an option to even partially compensate for the loss of other predators. From a few thousand animals in the early part of the twentieth century, Yellowstone's elk population ballooned to well over fifteen thousand by 1936. Concerned about deteriorating grasslands, the US National Park Service responded by culling varying numbers of surplus elk each winter. The neighbouring state of Montana began issuing cow licences to slow the population's growth.

By the late 1960s, elk numbers were down to about six thousand, but even that number was now too many. Over the previous decades, Yellowstone National Park's northern ranges had been devastated by overgrazing. Willows had virtually vanished from along the streams, eaten down repeatedly until they died, and with the loss of the willows, beavers vanished too. Without beavers, the streams eroded down into the silt floodplains that beaver dams had built up over the centuries, lowering the water table until the valleys dried out. Aspen groves, too, began to die back because every young aspen sprout encountered a set of elk incisors before it had a chance to grow tall enough to get beyond the reach of the hungry herds. As willow thickets vanished and aspen groves deteriorated, a host of other wildlife species that rely on deciduous habitats became rare or vanished too. So did ground-nesting grassland birds, because the grass never grew tall enough to shelter their nests.

Ecologists have long debated whether natural ecosystems are regulated from the bottom up – that is, by the availability of vegetation that supports the grazing animals that feed the predators – or from the top down, by predators that reduce the numbers of herbivorous animals, which in turn releases the vegetation from grazing pressure. The US National Park Service, for much of the twentieth century, implicitly accepted the bottom-up theory. That's why they slaughtered elk – to reduce overgrazing of the park's vegetation. Of course, this was in the days before ecology got much airplay, so the argument in support of culling elk was based on the now discredited range management concept of "carrying capacity."

Images of rangers surrounded with piles of dead elk, however, generated bad press for the National Park Service. By the 1960s, Yellowstone was at the bleeding edge of a lot of wildlife politics involving elk and grizzly bears. Senior managers in the Park Service commissioned panels of experts to review their management practices. One of the first panels, chaired by A. Starker Leopold, produced a report in 1963 entitled *Wildlife Management in the National Parks*. The Leopold Report triggered an end to elk culls and the beginning of the "natural regulation" era.

Within a few years, biologists were insisting that elk weren't too abundant after all. Top-down ecosystem regulation, at least implicitly, was the new gospel. There was no longer any need to worry about range condition, because predators and hard winters would regulate elk numbers if they got too abundant. That premise, unfortunately, discounted the absence of two of the most important pre-park-era elk predators: Aboriginal humans and wolves.

Three decades later, the elk herd was at twenty-three thousand and still growing! Hunters and hunting outfitters outside the park were delighted. The northern range, however, was an ecological wasteland.

Some park scientists tied themselves in knots in their efforts to prove that the massive herds weren't damaging the park's ecosystems. The grass was short, they argued, but it was still growing. Aspens were dying, but they were probably only there because of an accident of history; it actually was normal for the Yellowstone plateau to have fewer aspens. It might look like the streams and rivers were filling with silt from heavily grazed grassland pastures, but that was only anecdotal. Further research, the scientists said, might well prove that there was no problem at all. Beavers? They were probably never common on the northern range anyway.

And on and on ... the 1997 National Park Service publication *Yellowstone's Northern Range: Complexity and Change in a Wildland Ecosystem* makes embarrassing reading today. It's one of history's best examples of the dangers of politicizing science. Agency biologists seemed to be twisting themselves into knots trying to justify bureaucratic policies that were just plain ecologically wrong.

While Yellowstone's elk herds were devouring the world's first national park, however, change was in the wind. In 1973 the United States Congress declared the grey wolf an endangered species under their new Endangered Species Act. Unlike the weak-soup Species at Risk Act that Canada finally, belatedly, put in place two decades later, the ESA has serious teeth. Once a species earns a listing under the ESA, the US government is obligated to take meaningful action to recover it to a viable population status on its former range.

In the case of the wolf, that meant bringing it back to the western US. This was, politically, no easy task. Cattle interests had asserted a virtual stranglehold on the west's public lands and its congressional delegations, and they had no interest in sharing the landscape with an animal that, only a few short decades earlier, they had persuaded the federal government to exterminate.

The ESA, however, is federal law, and most of the western US is federal land that was never ceded to the states. Public sympathy was strongly on the side of the wolves. Public lands ranchers soon turned out to be big fish in a small pond. With the eyes of the entire American nation turned on the overgrazed rangelands they had controlled for decades, ranchers were suddenly vulnerable. Their pet congressmen and senators were outnumbered. The wolves won.

In 1995 and 1996, trappers in central BC and the Alberta foothills found themselves in the remarkable position of being asked to trap wolves but keep them alive for export to the US. The going price was US$2,000 per wolf – a lot more than the $400 they could get for the hide. For the wolves, it must have been an experience not unlike alien body-snatching. Having been chased down by helicopter and netted from the air, or trapped with specially modified neck snares, the wolves were drugged, dewormed, treated for any injuries, crated and transported by truck to airports for shipping to the United States. Waking to the flash of cameras and the sound of proud speeches, they were then turned out into large fenced enclosures in a strange landscape just saturated with the smell of elk.

After being held a while in enclosures to become comfortable in their new surroundings, the thirty-one wolves in Yellowstone National Park were set free. Another thirty-five were turned loose without any initial coddling into the large wilderness areas of central Idaho. They had arrived in wolf heaven. Literally thousands of elk, none of which had ever seen a wolf before, surrounded them. The naive ungulates were finally about to learn what it means to be a real elk. Their halcyon days of lounging around and lazily grazing favourite meadows down to the soil were over.

Wolf heaven – the greater Yellowstone ecosystem – supported as many as twenty-five thousand elk in the late 1990s. It didn't take long for the elk to relearn forgotten life skills, like moving frequently, watching constantly and avoiding open country until forced there by winter snows. Even so, with that much available prey, the wolves thrived. Conventional wisdom about each wolf pack having only one litter of pups each year went out the door as the nouveau-riche newcomers produced two and even three litters per pack each year, their fecundity no longer limited by scarcity of food.

By the end of the first decade of the twenty-first century, Yellowstone National Park was home to ten wolf packs totalling just under a hundred wolves. And that was just the national park.

The *2010 Annual Report on Rocky Mountain Wolf Recovery*, distributed by the US Fish and Wildlife Service on behalf of an interagency team, tallied over 500 wolves in the Greater Yellowstone Ecosystem, and more than 730 in the central Idaho recovery area. Reintroduction of the timber wolf to Yellowstone and central Idaho had been an overwhelming success.

Even though Idaho and Montana now have annual wolf hunting seasons, the wolf population continues to expand. Hunting may even have helped, since it fragments packs, something that can trigger increases both to reproduction and dispersal. Wolves from Idaho and Yellowstone have established new packs in Washington and Utah and sent wandering pioneers as far afield as Colorado and California.

Too Many Wolves

Wolves nearly vanished from Alberta, or at least the southern half of the province, twice during historical times. In the late 1800s, wolfers out of Fort Benton and other frontier outposts along the Missouri River travelled north in search of wolf pelts into the prairie regions of what would later become Alberta. The wolfers would shoot a bison, elk or even an old horse and lace the carcass liberally with strychnine, a broad-spectrum poison that causes its victims to die in painful convulsions. So effectively did they fill the landscape with poison that by the beginning of the twentieth century not only were wolves extirpated from the plains, but scavenging animals like the swift fox, raven and magpie were also gone.

In the forested areas farther north, trappers used both poisons and leg-hold traps to kill wolves. Wolves that managed to keep their skins intact still faced hard times. It was a long way between meals. Beavers had been trapped out by the 1880s. Traders, farmers, miners and other settlers, having killed the last of the region's bison, went on to decimate elk, deer and moose populations too. Many of the hoofed animals that survived the uncontrolled subsistence and market hunting of early Albertans died during devastating winters in the late 1880s, and again in 1906/07.

John Gunson, for many years the province's chief carnivore biologist, published a history of wolf management in 1992. He attributed the rarity of wolves in the early twentieth century to widespread use of poisons and severe declines in prey animal populations.

Even so, by the 1920s and 1930s, wolf numbers were recovering and wolves again ranged throughout the foothills and north through the boreal forest. The province of Alberta, struggling to survive the economic depression of the 1930s, eliminated its long-established bounty on wolves, removing an economic incentive from rural Alberta that was, in any case, becoming depopulated as a result of drought.

Hunters and farmers began increasingly to

complain about wolf depredations on livestock and wild game in the 1940s. Men and guns alike were scarce in the woods during the Second World War. In response, the government began to promote the use of neck snares – a highly effective trapping technique for wolves – by registered trappers. Provincial agricultural and problem-wildlife staff adopted the highly lethal "coyote-getter" to kill wolves and coyotes in 1950. The government even distributed strychnine to local fish and game clubs.

Alberta Fish and Game Association "Predator Chair" G. Riach, in his 1953 report to the AFGA annual convention, wrote:

> Our wolf situation is serious from all over the game areas, and there is undoubted evidence of inroads into our game wealth. Take a look at the map: see how we are squeezed by national parks on our entire boundary on the west, and by Buffalo Park on the N.W.T. in the North. These vast areas are breeding places of wolves and predators, and it's a wonder we have any worthwhile game left. We must insist on controls immediately. It's practically

of no use to poison, trap or kill cougars and
wolves if the balance of nature theorists are
permitted to govern.

Don Meredith and Duane Radford, in their history compilation *Conservation Pride and Passion:
The Alberta Fish and Game Association, 1908–2008*,
point out that many of that generation of fish-
and-gamers had grown up in an era when game
was very scarce. Their experience gave them no
reason to imagine that wild ungulates would ever
be common again, so their prejudices were under-
standable. They were sure that the slowly recovering big-game herds would be devastated if wolves
were free to hunt the few remaining animals day
and night, all year long.

How scarce were deer and elk? Heavy frontier
exploitation of the region's wildlife herds for food
had been followed by massive waves of rural settle-
ment in the early 1900s. By the 1930s, deer were
virtually unknown east of the Rocky Mountains:
people had eaten them all. Small pockets of deer
and elk survived in unroaded mountain valleys
and the large foothill ranches of western Alberta,
but even as late as the mid-1950s there was no legal

hunting season for deer east of Highway 2. At the 1954 AFGA convention in Calgary, Hunting Chair J. E. Carr went so far as to propose that "if we are to have really good deer hunting again in Alberta, I think we should plant several small herds of white-tail deer in our Foothills country."

Had he only known – within three decades, the province would be swarming with them.

The hunting groups didn't have to worry about wolves much longer. Faced with an outbreak of rabies in skunks and foxes between 1952 and 1956, the province launched a major disease eradication program that involved distributing poisoned baits across the entire settled landscape of the province. Wolves weren't part of the rabies problem, but they ate the baits anyway. Gunson and his colleague John Stelfox estimated that more than 80 per cent of Alberta's wolf population died during that campaign. They were virtually eradicated south of the North Saskatchewan River and survived only as small, isolated packs in the most remote mountain valleys farther north.

Meantime, populations of caribou, elk and deer were rebounding. The commercial trade in wild meat had ended decades earlier. Subsistence hunting also declined as the young province's economy grew. Faced with fewer two- and four-legged predators and spared the long, severe winters that had decimated wild ungulates and domestic livestock alike around the turn of the twentieth century, wildlife populations boomed.

By the end of the century, large herds of elk had become a scourge for foothills ranchers. Rural depopulation, which began in the 1930s and continues today, contributed to the improved prospects for deer in prairie and parkland areas. So did the spread of aspen and other woody habitats with the extinction first of bison and then, to a large degree, of prairie fires. Frost-resistant strains of alfalfa, developed in the 1960s, enabled central Alberta farmers to plant semi-permanent forage crops that benefited not just their own cattle herds but the region's exploding populations of white-tailed deer too. And after the province of Alberta began employing professional biologists in the early 1950s, successive science-based refinements to hunting regulations enabled the elk and deer herds along the Rocky Mountain east slopes to recover and grow.

By the end of the twentieth century, Alberta hunters were enjoying better big-game hunting than ever before. Wolves, being hunters like us, naturally thrived too, at least in the parts of the province where they could stay out of sight of roads.

Regardless of how good the hunting has become, however, at the first sight of a wolf scat on a cow trail or a long-legged Lobo loping out of sight into the pines, the word usually passes quickly from one hunter to the next: there are too many wolves.

In some places – caribou country, for example – that may even be true. If so, we made it that way.

The End of Caribou?

Those who find it easy to stereotype hunters as self-serving Bambi-killers should note that during the same period when the AFGA was demanding a wolf kill to increase the game herds, they were also asking government to close some hunting seasons entirely. Carr's 1954 report was one of several during that era to raise a red flag about dwindling caribou herds: "Our caribou population is very low. While this association has favoured a closed season on these animals for several years now, nothing has been done about it, and if some action is not taken soon, these beautiful animals are going to disappear entirely from Alberta. A closed season is a must."

The AFGA had briefly gotten their wish in 1948, but the government reopened the season in 1950. Caribou numbers continued to decline, and in 1979 the AFGA renewed its call for a closed season. Finally, in 1981, with caribou herds near Grande Cache dropping precipitously, the province closed the caribou season for good. Within four years, however, caribou were listed as threatened in Alberta.

Unfortunately, during that same decade the same government subsidized massive expansion of the forest industry. Roads, clearcuts and landscape fragmentation have far more devastating effects on caribou than hunters ever did. Carr's dire prediction may yet come true – but not because of hunters.

Beginning in the late 1950s and accelerating through the ensuing decades, Alberta's foothills and boreal forests have been ravaged beyond belief by the oil and gas industry and massive

logging operations. Successive Alberta governments have not only cheered the destruction
along – whenever it seemed likely to abate, they
subsidized it with relaxed regulations or direct
cash infusions.

Just as an earlier generation of Albertans grew
up thinking deer and elk would never be abundant
again, subsequent generations of Albertans have
grown up thinking that shattered landscapes,
eroding cutlines and stripped forests are just the
normal way of things. Both generations were
wrong.

The fragmented remains of western and northern Alberta's forest landscapes nonetheless provide
great habitat for the once-rare white-tailed deer,
elk and moose. Second-growth forest is full of the
willows, herbs and poplars they eat. In most parts
of the region, there are still enough mature forest
stands to give them shelter from bad weather and
camo-clad hunters in trucks.

With other ungulates more abundant than
hunters in early Alberta could ever have imagined,
caribou, unfortunately, came out the loser. Not
only is their habitat under steadily increasing assault by loggers and drilling crews, but it has more

wolves than ever before, their numbers boosted by booming elk, deer and moose populations.

Caribou are ice age animals. They thrive in cold climates and marginal habitats where other hoofed animals fail. Their large hooves support small bodies, minimizing the amount that they sink in winter snow. They eat both ground lichens, cratering down through the early winter snow to unearth them, and tree lichens, which they can browse at steadily increasing heights as the snow pack deepens. Lichens grow slowly. That's why old forest landscapes are essential to caribou. And lichen is neither a highly nutritious nor a fast-growing food source. That's why even large tracts of undisturbed landscape support relatively small numbers of caribou.

Their scarcity, even in the best of times, makes caribou particularly sensitive to predation. They solve that problem by spending their winters in deep snow, where wolves and cougars are reluctant to go. While predators hunt elk, deer and moose in the shallow-snow pockets along river valleys and ridge systems, the caribou are back in the dark forest of the muskegs and old spruce forests, standing up to their bellies in soft snow while munching on coarse bear-hair lichens that festoon the branches of aging trees.

At least, that's how it used to be. Increasingly, however, oil and gas companies have cut seismic lines or well roads into those once-remote fastnesses. Even after the companies leave, snowmobilers and off-road riders take over the abandoned roads, packing down the snow so that wolves can easily penetrate areas that deep snow once excluded them from. It's worth their while, because caribou are easier to kill than elk and deer, whose evolutionary history has given them a lot more exposure to wolf predation, giving rise to much stronger predator defences. Besides, logging companies have broken up a lot of the old forest based on a standard operating principle that applies in every Forest Management Area in the province: log the old stuff first. A wolf following a snowmobile track into old-growth caribou habitat stands a good chance of finding new clearcuts with enough moose or whitetails to hold it there until it kills a caribou or two.

Climate change is a further challenge for Alberta's more southerly herds of caribou. Today's snow packs are often shallower and comprised of denser snow than was the norm even fifty years ago. Dense, shallow snow is less of an impediment to wolves than deep, fluffy stuff. Even without the help of industrial roads and the snowmobilers who play on them, wolves can get around better than before.

Cold-adapted and snow-dependent caribou survived well into the Holocene – the post-ice-age epoch in which modern human societies developed – because their ice age habitats persisted in northern and mountain regions even while the rest of the landscape turned into elk, bison and deer country. The Holocene is really an interglacial period, a warm spell between major continental glaciations. All other things being equal, there would be a good chance of another ice advance. The deep-snow world of the caribou would expand again.

But during this particular inter-glacial, human populations and technology exploded. We are burning fossil fuels at rates the earth has never experienced before. Fossil fuels – oil, coal, gas – are derived from carbon that got locked into the rocks beneath the earth's surface over millions of years.

By pulling all that carbon to the surface and burning it, we are filling the atmosphere with carbon dioxide in unprecedented concentrations.

Carbon dioxide is a greenhouse gas; it lets light radiation – sunlight – through but holds heat radiation in. As the surface of the earth warms each summer, the changing atmosphere now traps heat that used to be reflected back into space. Barring something spectacular – an immense volcanic eruption that fills the atmosphere with dust for several years, a mass die-off of humans, or perhaps a meteor collision that has the same effect as a massive volcano – the spiralling effects of climate change are likely to move the Earth into a long-term warming trend that will spell the end to a lot of things, caribou included.

The trend has been evident for at least a century. Caribou used to live in northern Idaho and Montana, including the Flathead River valley west of Waterton. Most of those relict herds vanished before the beginning of the twentieth century.

The headwaters of the Red Deer and Clearwater Rivers still had caribou through the first half of the twentieth century. When Alberta built its Forestry Trunk Road through the high foothills in the 1960s, however, those caribou became vulnerable to poachers. The late Henry Stelfox, one of the first game guardians in the area west of Rocky Mountain House, kept detailed notes of his experiences, which his family later released in a self-published book entitled *Rambling Thoughts of a Wandering Fellow: A Natural History of Wildlife, Native Peoples, Homesteading, and Conservation in Western Alberta: 1906–1968*. Stelfox described seeing his first caribou near Peppers Creek, an area now traversed not only by the Forestry Trunk Road but also by a mishmash of oil and gas well roads, logging roads and off-road vehicle trails. Those caribou are long gone, just as others vanished from the North Saskatchewan River farther north after construction of the David Thompson Highway.

A small relict herd survived farther upstream, in the remote alpine meadows and timberline forests of Banff National Park. When we did a wildlife inventory of the mountain parks in the late 1970s, there were about twenty in that herd. By the early twentieth century, predation by wolves and bears had reduced that number to five. In the winter of 2009, all five remaining caribou died in an avalanche near Molar Pass. And that was the end of Banff's caribou.

Jasper's caribou will be the next to go. Once famous for caribou herds that ranged the Skyline Trail and Poboktan/Jonas Pass areas in summer and often wintered along the Icefields Parkway near Jonas Creek or, in alternate years, along the Maligne valley road, the Maligne Range had fewer than twenty surviving caribou by 2012. High numbers of elk and deer in the nearby Athabasca and Brazeau valleys support a robust wolf population. The wolves follow ploughed roads and ski tracks into the high country each winter. There, they kill caribou. Parks Canada has known about the problem for at least two decades but has managed only weak half-measures to keep wolves from exploiting human travel-ways into caribou country.

The Maligne herd will likely be gone within a decade – unimaginable once, but inevitable when rapid climate change and weak conservation policies collide.

Even though woodland caribou are a threatened species in Canada, Environment Canada dithered for years about how to protect them. Any meaningful measures would involve securing the last remaining old-growth forest landscapes and reforesting the roads and clearcuts that fragment much of what used to be caribou habitat. That would mean butting heads with provincial governments that profit from forest, oil and gas revenues. *A Recovery Strategy for the Woodland Caribou, Boreal Population (*Rangifer tarandus caribou*) in Canada*, belatedly released in 2011, called for aggressive wolf control to keep predation mortality levels low until habitat can be restored.

There's biological sense to that idea. In their changing world, caribou are easy prey for wolves. But the flaw, of course, is that the draft recovery strategy includes no substantive measures to restore habitat – just more planning. If industry continues to fragment forested landscapes, Canada will lose its woodland caribou no matter how many wolves we slaughter.

National parks might save Jasper's threatened herds – but only if Parks Canada makes hard, long-overdue decisions about closing winter roads and directing ski and snowshoe traffic away from caribou refuge areas in deep-snow habitats. In spite of small, experimental first steps, so far they've given tourism priority over caribou. Caribou don't lobby park ministers or write letters to newspapers.

Outside the national parks, in places like the Little Smoky River valley north of Hinton, other caribou herds are on the verge of blinking out forever. Their last intact habitats are under siege from a society that seems incapable of leaving anything alone. If we believe that there is a future and that it matters, then there's really no need to develop the whole boreal landscape, nor to extract all its timber resources, oil and gas in one human lifetime. But that seems to be the plan – to the extent that there is any plan. Restraint, humility and thrift – rare virtues in the world of resource development and anathema to the free-market extremists who increasingly control economic policy – offer the only real hope for wilderness-dependent species like the woodland caribou.

It is obviously counterproductive to continually create ideal habitat for the deer and moose that wolves eat, and then try to control wolf numbers– but this appears to be the preferred option for government land managers. And that's why, noble and self-sacrificing as the Alberta Fish and Game Association was in calling for an end to caribou hunting, its leadership will likely prove to have been in vain. Land managers and their political masters are making Alberta's boreal a great place for wolves and a lousy place for caribou.

I remember seeing a bumper sticker once that said it all: "It's the Habitat, Stupid!"

It wasn't on the bumper of an Alberta Forest Service truck.

Not Enough Wolves

Dead Trees, Dry Ponds

The willows are getting tall again along the Vermilion Lakes. It may not be long until the beavers are back too. That would be good; it's been a while.

At the age of fifty-five, and with a bum leg, Hubert Green wasn't able to go to war as so many other Canadian men were doing in 1940. Instead, he hired on with the Dominion Parks Service as a special wildlife warden in Banff National Park. There, he became responsible for compiling reports on the status of various kinds of park wildlife, offering biological advice on their management, and educating the public about them.

Before arriving in Banff, Green had gotten to know legendary English-born conservationist Grey Owl at Riding Mountain National Park. Having seen how popular Grey Owl's half-tamed beavers were with visiting tourists, Green was soon advertising evening beaver shows at the Vermilion Lakes, just west of the national park townsite.

All three lakes had active beaver lodges, and there were dams along the small stream channels joining them. So many beavers lived in the lower Bow valley that locals complained that the beaver ponds were making it impossible to enjoy the place because of the mosquitoes they produced. In response, park wardens destroyed 235 beaver dams in the lower Bow River valley in 1943 alone. Even so, each summer evening, beavers continued to appear along the edges of the Vermilion Lakes, where they cut willows and aspen stems, sinking them in underwater food caches or using them to repair leaky dams. As often as not, Hubert Green would be there waiting with a group of fascinated tourists, ready to explain the ways of beavers and how their wetland-building activities affected the natural history of the park.

By 1944, Green was cutting aspen tops close to town and taking them to the popular beaver viewing locations. Supplies were getting sparse along the lakeshore itself. Beavers have a habit of eating themselves out of house and home, but the growing abundance of elk didn't help either. Each winter, when beavers were feeding from their sunken stashes beneath the blanketing ice and snow, hundreds of elk gathered in the low-elevation Bow valley to escape the deep snows at higher elevations. There, the growing herds browsed the new growth from aspens, willows and other deciduous shrubs. When snows grew deep or browse got sparse, they stripped green bark from the trees.

Prior to the area becoming Canada's first national park, elk had been rare in the Bow valley. Elk were among the easiest of prey for resident Aboriginal hunters and the wolves and other predators that ranged the Rocky Mountain Front Ranges. Archaeological digs have proven that elk were already scarce even before market hunters eradicated the last of them in the late 1800s.

By Green's time, the Stoney Nakoda First Nation had been excluded from its traditional hunting grounds for almost half a century. Wolves and cougars, too, were scarce in those mid-twentieth-century years, much to Green's disapproval. His reports recommended an end to the established practice of predator-killing by park wardens. Being ahead of his time, he was ignored.

Park authorities set free an initial thirty-two elk in 1916 to restore the park herds. They imported about two hundred more from Yellowstone over the next three years. The ungrazed vegetation was lush and predators were few; within two decades, elk numbered in the thousands. Just like Yellowstone, Banff eventually had to start culling its elk herd to reduce range damage. Park wardens conducted the first elk slaughter in 1941, the year that Green began his beaver talks at Vermilion Lakes. The largest slaughter – 352 elk – was in 1946. By then, beavers were already beginning to decline for lack of food. Elk were eating it before beavers could.

The controversial elk culls didn't stop the growth of the herds. Through the late twentieth century, Banff National Park's Bow valley – like Yellowstone – became a poor and deteriorating place. Most of the surviving aspens were old and unhealthy, their trunks black and scarred as high as an elk could reach – the result of hungry elk tearing the bark away with their incisors to eat the green inner bark. Aspen stands had virtually no shrubby understory and no young aspen sprouts at all. Adjacent grasslands were grazed down to stubble. Beaver and moose, out-competed for forage, became rare. Without beaver dams, wetlands dried or shrank. Ground-nesting birds became increasingly scarce because the sparse vegetation cover left by hungry elk was not enough to hide their nests from predators. Other species that rely on tall willows for habitat, like the song sparrow, Wilson's warbler and willow flycatcher, also became scarce, because the only surviving willows were stunted sprouts that elk browsed back each year.

There were just too many elk. It was the same story all across the mountain west.

Biologist Cristina Eisenberg has no doubt that western ecosystems are regulated from the top down. She has studied trophic cascades in Banff, Yellowstone and other western national parks, as well as private lands in Utah, Colorado and elsewhere. Her book *The Wolf's Tooth* chronicles several examples of landscapes whose ecological diversity went into a tailspin during the twentieth century as ungulate populations, freed of effective predation, climbed to all-time highs.

Cristina points out that it is not just the number of elk, deer or other grazing animals in the landscape that matters; it's how they behave. Ungulates that live with predators occupy what she describes as a "landscape of fear." They move frequently, often adopting seasonal migration strategies to escape predation, whereas wolves are tied to their dens by young pups that aren't yet as mobile as the adult pack members. Ungulates that don't need to dodge predators can become lazy and sedentary, parking themselves in the most productive parts of the landscape, where they overgraze the available forage until their preferred food plants begin to die.

With the return of wolves to Banff and, a couple decades later, to Yellowstone, the dumbing-down of national park ecosystems appears to have been reversed. Banff's elk population has dropped from several thousand to only a few hundred. They move frequently. Vegetation is recovering. Grass species like rough fescue, once not even known to occur in the park, have become unexpectedly common.

Yellowstone's herds were vastly larger than Banff's and have dropped somewhat less pre-cipitously. Even so, young aspens are reappearing along the edges of that national park's aging, decadent groves, as they are in Banff. Willows are rising above wet sedge meadows where they were once only a fading memory. Savannah sparrows are successfully raising broods of young again, sheltered by uneaten grass clumps, while aspen-loving songbird species again greet the mountain dawn from unbrowsed twigs nearby.

That's in the places with wolves. Other western landscapes continue to deteriorate. There are still no wolf tracks on the trails of Colorado's Rocky Mountain National Park. Its hyper-abundant elk – now infected with chronic wasting disease – continue to devour the last surviving aspen and willow stands in the park even as more northerly parks recover.

In the early twenty-first century, the US Forest Service began sounding alarms about a phenom-enon for which foresters coined the term "Sudden Aspen Decline." Aspen stands all across the west were dying back. In 2008 alone, according to the Forest Service, more than 17 per cent of all the aspen stands in Colorado were affected by the sudden loss of their foliage and increased tree mortality.

Aspen reproduces from seed only rarely, when conditions are ideal. Once established, however, aspens can last for centuries because of their habit of sprouting new, young growth from their roots. A few sprouts come up every year, but what really stimulates a huge flush of new growth is any disturbance that kills off the adult trees, cutting the flow of growth-inhibiting hormones to the roots. Most of the west's aspen groves were likely established centuries ago but have been renewed repeatedly by fire, wind-throw, avalanching, beavers or other natural disturbance processes. Severe droughts can kill adult trees too, but the next wet cycle enables the roots once again to renew the forest.

The Forest Service blames Sudden Aspen Decline on a combination of drought and insects and, true to its culture, prescribes more logging as the solution. Logging, like other disturbances, does in fact trigger aspen roots to re-sprout. But the new sprouts are at exactly the right height to feed elk, deer and cattle. And elk, in particular, search out new aspen sprouts.

Wardens used fire, instead of logging, to renew aspen forests in Banff National Park during the 1990s. To their chagrin, they found that they had actually hastened the demise of the stands. Elk, still abundant at the time, quickly descended on the new growth and ate it into oblivion. If the "more logging" prescription gets applied in Colorado and elsewhere in the west, the same thing will happen wherever unnaturally high numbers of elk persist, especially if there are no wolves to discourage them from lingering in the logged stands.

One reason elk populations in Colorado and elsewhere are at or near all-time highs is that the most abundant predator left to control their numbers is the licensed sport hunter. Elk hunters only kill elk during a short period each fall, and only in places that actually permit hunting. Private landowners have placed large tracts of private land out of bounds for public hunting. Elk quickly learn to retreat into those places. There, they wait out the hunting season – while browsing down the local aspens and willows – only to spread out across the rest of the beaten-down countryside when the hunting season ends.

The future across most of the Rocky Mountain west, then, will likely involve more elk, fewer aspens, declining populations of ground-nesting birds and those that rely on lush deciduous vegetation, more washed-out beaver dams and – if the US Forest Service solution is applied – more logging to destroy the surviving aspen stands. It will not be the fine place we imagine, or remember.

Except, of course, where the wolves have come home.

Mad Deer Disease

Canada's federal and provincial governments set up an expert panel in the early twenty-first century to look at a frightening new disease that game farmers had inadvertently imported into Saskatchewan. The conclusion of their 2004 final report, *Chronic Wasting Disease in Canadian Wildlife: An Expert Opinion on the Epidemiology and Risks to Wild Deer*, was blunt: "The emergence of chronic wasting disease, a transmissible spongiform encephalopathy potentially affecting mule deer, white-tailed deer and elk, is arguably the most important issue in the management of free-living cervids in North America."

Chronic wasting disease, or CWD, is also called mad deer disease. It is very closely related to the notorious mad cow disease and to Creutzfeldt-Jakob

Disease, which causes always-fatal brain deterioration in human beings.

Unlike diseases spread by bacteria or viruses that invade the bodies of their hosts, CWD and other kinds of transmissible spongiform encephalopathy (TSE) are produced by prions: tiny, deformed proteins that replicate inside the animal and spread through the blood system to actively attack brain and neural tissue. It's called a "spongiform encephalopathy" because the brains of its victims are so full of holes that they look like sponges by the time they die.

They always die.

The "transmissible" part of the name comes from the fact that the disease can be transmitted to other animals. In the case of deer and elk, prions transfer from one individual to another through urine, saliva and the unfortunate habit ungulates have of chewing on shed antlers and the bones of dead animals. Animals that crowd together while feeding and drinking from common troughs are particularly good at passing on the disease. Prions are tough little things: even long after the last bone or antler fragment is gone, they persist in the soil. Neither freezing nor cooking will destroy them.

CWD is something new under the sun. Nobody had ever seen it until 1967. That year, deer and elk in a research facility in Fort Collins, Colorado, began to display symptoms. They drooled and urinated frequently, became emaciated, uncoordinated and increasingly listless, and staggered glazed-eyed around their enclosures. Finally they lay down and died.

The research facility had previously held domestic sheep infected with scrapie, another TSE disease, so some of the researchers suspected that the deer had somehow become infected with scrapie. Indeed, they might have: the new disease had to originate somewhere. But experience in the past had been that TSEs were species-specific. It took another decade before the late Dr. Beth Williams was able to prove conclusively that what was killing the research animals was, in fact, a new form of TSE.

The new disease soon appeared in wild mule deer outside the facility, likely spread by nose contact through the tall fence that enclosed the captive deer. Even then, CWD might have been contained to the foothills and plains around Boulder if it hadn't been for a wave of neo-conservative

zeal that swept the state and provincial governments of western North America during the late
twentieth century. The neo-cons put their faith in
unregulated commerce, disdained expert advice
and dismissed many of the great policy achievements of the twentieth century as outdated at best
and nanny-state social engineering at worst. Their
small-government libertarian rhetoric played well
with large blocs of don't-tread-on-me western
voters. It still does.

Barely a century earlier, US president Theodore
Roosevelt and Canadian prime minister Wilfrid
Laurier had set in place one of the most suc-
cessful systems of wildlife conservation in the
world – one that brought many species of North
American wildlife from the brink of extinction
to widespread abundance. One of the central
tenets of their unique North American system of
conservation was the prohibition of commercial
markets for, and trade in, wildlife. Wildlife markets had brought the sea mink, passenger pigeon
and Labrador duck to extinction and, by the
early years of the twentieth century, had even put
white-tailed deer and elk on the ropes. With trade
prohibited, wildlife numbers rebounded.

The new right-wing governments smugly tossed that principle out the door in the 1980s and 1990s. In fact, they reversed it. One after another, American states and Canadian provinces legalized the commercial culture and sale of captive elk and deer. They did it ostensibly in the name of economic diversification, but it proved in reality to be a pyramid scheme. Game-farming boosters said it would buffer farmers from ups and downs in market prices for conventional livestock while enabling them to generate revenue from marginal farmland – once all the native wildlife had been fenced out, of course.

Darrell Rowledge is one of Canada's leading authorities on the history of CWD. His exhaustively researched book *No Accident ... Public Policy and Chronic Wasting Disease in Canada* argues that the governments of the day were too enthusiastic to bother with due diligence. Expert studies warning about the risks of disease transfer and economic failure got buried. Politicians and bureaucrats insisted game farming was an agricultural matter, not a wildlife one, so the concerns of biologists and wildlife groups got short shrift. And so the plague was unleashed.

Game farms began to pop up everywhere. The hopeful owners went shopping for deer and elk. Political insiders who were the first out of the gate profited richly from the sale of breeding stock. Then the markets for the products of captive wildlife – deer velvet and venison – crashed. Countless family farmers who had trusted their government agriculture departments were left holding the bag.

By then it was far too late to stop CWD.

The Fort Collins research facility had shipped some of its mule deer to the Denver Zoo. The zoo, in turn, sold animals to private game farms and zoos. A deer that it sold to the Toronto Zoo subsequently began to show symptoms of CWD and was destroyed. That should have put up a red flag, but it didn't. Other Fort Collins animals ended up in a South Dakota elk farm. That farm later shipped elk north to Saskatchewan and Alberta as seed stock for their new game-farming industry.

Darrell Rowledge quotes an epidemiologist from the US National Institutes of Health: "People ask how this disease is spreading, and I say by truck."

A lot of trucks moved a lot of deer and elk before sick animals began to turn up on game farms all across North America. CWD can take years to incubate in an infected animal before symptoms appear. Many shipments of game-farm animals were never properly documented, making the task of figuring out the disease's back-trail that much more of a challenge for Canada's expert panel.

According to the panel's report, the first Canadian case turned up on a Saskatchewan game farm in 1996, in a captive elk trucked across the border from South Dakota several years earlier. Two years later, the disease appeared on a second game farm in the same area, near Lloydminster. By 2000, it had been confirmed on forty Saskatchewan game farms and three more in Alberta.

In spite of advice from worried biologists, epidemiologists and hunting groups who had lost the battle to ban captive herds, no jurisdiction anywhere had required that game farms be double-fenced. It became common, especially during the fall breeding season, for wild local animals to touch noses with sick captive ones through game farm fences. So it came as no surprise to anyone but government authorities when, in November 2000, a hunter killed Canada's first CWD-infected deer near the contaminated game farms.

CWD had spread into the wild. In subsequent years, the disease exploded throughout the high-density white-tailed and mule deer populations near Swift Current, Saskatchewan, and all along the boundary area between Alberta and Saskatchewan. It will almost certainly arrive in Calgary, Red Deer and Edmonton within this decade.

It wasn't the first time CWD had gone feral. The original Fort Collins infection had also spread from captive animals into the area's wild mule deer and elk, and northern Colorado remains the epidemic's epicentre. Dr. Michael Miller, at that time one of the lead researchers into CWD and one of the experts appointed to Canada's expert panel, reported in testimony before the US Congress in 2002:

> The most intensively affected area extends from the Laramie Mountains in Wyoming south to the northern Front Range in Colorado. In this area, average infection rates exceed 10 per cent in sampled mule deer. Surveys have been conducted over the last five years in other parts of Colorado and Wyoming, as well as in portions of a number of nearby and distant states and provinces....

> With a few notable exceptions … none of
> these surveys have revealed other foci of
> CWD presently exist in free-ranging cervids.

The exceptions to which he referred were all in the vicinity of game farms.

None of those exceptions was in wolf country.

Wolves have been gone from the Fort Collins area for almost a century. The absence of wolves helped ensure that, once CWD had spread into wild herds,. its further spread was assured. Infected animals, which can shed infectious prions for months, freely spread the pestilence before finally succumbing to the disease.

Wolves hunt by coursing the landscape in search of prey, and then testing the animals they find to see if they can detect any weaknesses or vulnerability. Their senses are exquisitely attuned to body language or behaviour that indicates a deer or elk is not thriving, even when that same animal seems perfectly fine to human observers. Some of the animals that wolves kill are healthy, fit adults who just happened to have a bad day, perhaps by being surprised at close quarters or chased into a snowdrift. But countless studies have shown that their coursing-and-testing hunting style results in wolves most commonly killing the weak and the vulnerable. Those can be young animals, very old animals, animals that have suffered accidental injuries ... or sick ones.

CWD is a disease of the nervous system. It affects its victims' ability to perceive danger, to coordinate their movements and to make good instinctive choices. In other words, it's perfectly suited for making animals vulnerable to wolves. And wolves are the ideal solution for culling those sick animals early, before their disease has progressed to the point where they are dripping prions all over the landscape to infect other animals – or before a human hunter shoots one and takes the meat home to feed his or her family.

That risk is a serious one. In Britain, the similar mad cow disease spread from supermarket beef to several dozens of humans, all of whom then died from brain deterioration. Although most government disease specialists insist that there is no proof that mad deer disease can jump to humans in the same way, none will go on record as saying it won't. In Saskatchewan, Alberta, Wisconsin and other places where CWD has spread into wild herds, hunting brochures advise hunters not to handle meat with bare hands or to eat the meat of untested animals. The risk is real.

Meantime, ironically, game farms continue to sell meat and antler velvet to consumers without any cautionary messages. No less ironically, the great free-market experiment failed: most game farms are now economically marginal – unless they have diseased animals, for which they can collect lucrative taxpayer-funded compensation.

CWD is spreading inexorably, but it has yet to infect wild herds in regions where wolves could play a role in herd sanitation. Wolves have been absent for almost a century from the infected areas around Lloydminster and Swift Current. More recently, sick deer have turned up farther east near Nipawin and farther west along the Red Deer and South Saskatchewan River valleys – no wolves there, either.

Coyotes are common in those areas, and these smaller predators sometimes kill deer, especially in winter. Coyotes, however, are designed for and inclined toward smaller prey. They likely kill the odd sick animal, but they aren't nearly as efficient as their larger relatives.

Be that as it may, wolves won't likely get an opportunity to help soon. Three generations of farmers and ranchers have raised cattle, sheep and swine in the aspen parkland and northern prairie regions of Alberta and Saskatchewan since the last wolf died of strychnine poisoning there. Their fear and loathing for wolves is nearly universal.

Consequently, instead of the free services of a predator that is on duty 24/7, 365 days of the year, the strategy for controlling the spread of the disease has been to spend even more tax dollars on aerial gunning programs aimed at depleting the deer herds, and to offer licensed sport hunters free extra tags if they will kill extra deer. There is no way of targeting sick animals – hunters, of course, prefer healthy ones – so the goofy solution is just to kill a bunch of deer.

That's why CWD – which continues to spread into Canada's once-healthy deer and elk herds – is here to stay. The goofy solution may be here to stay too, although Saskatchewan and Alberta have already scaled back their efforts in what seems to be a tacit admission of defeat. Certainly the helicopter gunship solution didn't stop the spread of the disease. Nor have the continuing CWD disaster

– or an earlier outbreak of tuberculosis in captive herds – shut down the game-farming industry.

Bad policy is as stubbornly resistant to eradication as is CWD.

Wilful negligence defines government policy on game farming and CWD as much today as it did when earlier governments first unleashed the disaster in the 1980s. In one of the most recent triumphs of conservative ideology over responsible government, Canada's federal government cut funding in 2012 to almost all prion research studies and ceased to compensate for or monitor the spread of the disease in captive herds or in the wild. Canada is blundering into a disease-ridden future, blindfolded.

The return of the wolf might be the last faint hope for parkland and prairie areas already infected with CWD. Given how unlikely that return is, however, the safest place for humans to hunt deer and elk for meat may soon be those parts of western Canada that still have plenty of wolves.

That will be a head-scratcher for the fish-and-game groups that spent more than a century lobbying government to get rid of those wolves.

Cattle Country Wolves

One day in early 1996, my eleven-year-old daughter announced that I was going to take her out looking for wolves. That presented a bit of a challenge: I knew that hunters, ranchers, trappers and accidents had killed virtually all the wolves near our home in Waterton Lakes National Park during the past few months. An estimated regional population of sixty had dwindled to perhaps ten or so, and those wary survivors inhabited remote country an hour's drive north. There was little point in looking for a wolf anywhere south of Banff.

Katie insisted, however, so we bundled up for the cold and set off into the winter woods on snowshoes.

When we cut coyote tracks, Katie agreed to make do with those. We found where the coyotes had hunted mice, frolicked in the snow and stopped to watch their back-trail. They knew we were following; as we returned along the half-frozen Waterton River, one yapped at us from the forest.

I yelped back. A moment later, two or three coyotes responded with a maniacal caterwauling. As the echoes faded, I thought I heard a deeper voice in the distance. Katie stood stock-still, listening. She looked up with a question on her face.

I tried a wolf howl. This time, the deep and mournful answer that came resonating through the winter afternoon was unmistakable.

"I told you we'd find one," Katie whispered.

Another howled, closer, somewhere in the tangle of cottonwoods and willows across the river. The two conversed: long-drawn moans interspersed with deep barks. We were just about to go looking for them when a third, deeper howl resonated out of the shadows right across the river.

We stood, surrounded by the hair-lifting chorus, for several minutes. Then, with the sun setting behind Mount Crandell, we hurried back to our vehicle and drove to where we could glass the area. In the patchy forest across the river, small bunches of white-tailed deer and two groups of bull elk were feeding in scattered meadows. Katie peered through our window-mounted spotting scope.

"The elk are running," she announced.

A grey wolf appeared at the edge of the aspens, trotting leisurely toward a cluster of elk. The elk ran a few metres then stopped as the wolf turned away. Now we could see a second grey wolf. Both rushed a group of deer. The deer darted away, then stopped and watched, white flags lifted. Again the wolves abandoned the pursuit.

We watched, enthralled, as the two greys and a large black wolf tested several more bunches in the fading evening light. At length, the wolves vanished into the aspens.

When we got home, Katie burst into the house to tell her mom and brothers the news. "Dad said we wouldn't find any wolves, but we did!"

Free-Trade Wolves

Only a year earlier, hunters and ranchers had virtually eradicated a pack that colonized the park in 1993 and subsequently raised two litters of pups. Katie's and my sighting was the first sign that more dispersers might have come north from Montana to reoccupy the range of the short-lived Belly River wolf pack.

Strychnine, snares and rifles had eradicated

wolves from the southern Rockies in the 1950s. Around 1960, however, rare stragglers began to appear. Most had likely found their way through mountain passes from BC's Elk and Flathead River valleys. By the early 1970s, when park wardens were reporting wolf tracks regularly along remote valleys in northern Banff National Park, ranchers in southwestern Alberta's foothills and BC's East Kootenay region were also spotting wolves regularly.

Dispersing wolves from northern BC and Alberta had established packs in the Kananaskis, Oldman, Elk and Flathead valleys by the early 1980s, but none survived for long in the narrow band of ranching country lying to the east of the Rockies and south of the Bow River. On the west side, wolves fared better, eventually dispersing south from BC to the Montana portion of the Flathead River valley. In 1986 Americans were thrilled to learn that, for the first time in half a century, wolves had denned and raised pups in the continental US.

Protected under the US Endangered Species Act, those colonizing wolves thrived. Within a decade, northern Montana had some thirteen or fourteen packs totalling more than a hundred wolves. In a sort of ecological free trade, young wolves dispersing from those Montana packs drifted north, back into Canada. There, after half a century of absence, they finally established three new packs in the southern Alberta foothills. Farther north, other wolves appeared in the Porcupine Hills, the Whaleback wilderness, and the upper Oldman and Highwood River valleys.

By late 1994, Alberta provincial biologists estimated that as many as sixty wolves occupied the game-rich southwestern corner of Alberta. Given that the province's official wolf management plan called for a population of fifty in the area, it was a success story – albeit a brief one.

It was the Americans who enabled us to learn as much as we did during the short-lived wolf boom of the mid-1990s. The US Fish and Wildlife Service (US FWS) had the lead, under the Endangered Species Act, in monitoring the wolves that had newly recolonized northern Montana. Starting with a number of wolves that researcher Diane Boyd had equipped with radio collars as part of her graduate research in the Flathead valley, the wolf recovery team adopted a protocol that aimed at having two to three radio-collared wolves in each new pack as soon as possible.

Early in 1993, I got a phone call from a US FWS biologist named Joe Fontaine. I was Waterton Lakes National Park's conservation biologist at the time. Joe introduced himself as the biologist in charge of monitoring their new Northern Continental Divide wolf population. We already knew that Salix, one of Diane Boyd's radio-collared wolves, was the alpha female of the new Belly River pack. Joe was seeking permission to trap two more wolves in the pack and fit them with radio collars. The wolves might be Canadian now, but the pack was still part of the US FWS study population.

Canada is different from the United States. The western US is primarily federal public land, but Canada's federal presence is limited to national parks, Indian reserves and military training areas. Since the Natural Resources Transfer Act transferred jurisdiction over public land, natural resources and most wildlife to the western provinces in 1930, the federal footprint in our west has been small. Federal agencies like

Parks Canada try to keep that footprint as light as possible too.

Waterton, at only 505 square kilometres, is too small to protect so wide-ranging an animal as the wolf. The Belly pack's daily travels took it into the Blood Timber Limit, a small outlying reserve of the Kainai (Blood) First Nation, as well as Alberta public lands and privately owned ranches. Wolves in our area could be legally shot and killed pretty much anywhere, anytime, except inside the national park – another big difference from the US.

My advice to Joe, consequently, was that he come up and meet the neighbours. He could make his pitch to all of them. I offered to work with the Waterton Biosphere Reserve Association to pull a couple of meetings together. The WBRA is a rancher-founded volunteer organization that promotes science and sustainable management in an IUCN biosphere reserve that includes Waterton Lakes National Park.

That was the beginning of a fascinating, if ultimately frustrating, foray into the human cultural landscape that wolves have so much difficulty navigating. Even we humans don't do too well in that landscape when discussion turns to wolves.

Larry Frith, a Twin Butte organic rancher, was chair of the Waterton Biosphere Reserve Association at the time. He and I jointly led two public information sessions in June 1994: one in Twin Butte, on the west side of the Waterton River, and the other at Mountain View, on the east side.

If the meetings taught us anything, it was that they were a mistake. In rural communities, people trust most those whom they already know. The guy in a suit or a government vehicle is not automatically viewed as a friend, especially if he invites you to a meeting. And especially if it's about wolves.

Larry Frith introduced the resource people at the head table. Joe Fontaine then explained what the US was doing on the wolf recovery front. He bent over backward to make it clear that their only interest in Canadian wolves was to monitor them, not to seek their protection. Richard Quinlan, the recently appointed head wildlife biologist for the Alberta Fish and Wildlife Service's southern Rocky Mountains and foothills region, then gave a presentation on the province's wolf management plan. While noting that the plan set a population target for southwestern Alberta of fifty wolves, he emphasized that there were no plans to change the province's very liberal wolf-killing regulations.

I then offered Parks Canada's perspective: we wanted to welcome wolves back into Waterton Lakes National Park and they would be rigorously protected there, but we understood the need for regional management that respected the interests of the neighbours. Then Larry opened the floor to questions. There were surprisingly few.

At both meetings, most of the fifty or so mostly male ranchers in attendance leaned back in their seats, legs fully extended and arms crossed, leaning over occasionally to mutter a few words to their neighbours. The asides were usually met with a short chuckle or a cynical shake of the head. I had a nagging sense that the body language was telling me something I didn't want to know.

The eye-opener came the day after the Mountain View meeting. A colleague, a rancher whose park job supplemented his income, collared me in my office. He hadn't been able to get to the meeting, so he'd asked one of his neighbours for an update.

"What's this I hear about you guys flying a bunch of wolves into the country?" he demanded.

"What?"

"You know. The ones you're stocking near Payne Lake. Where are you going to get fifty wolves, and why on earth would you put them at Payne Lake? Who is this Fontaine guy, anyway, and who's paying for the helicopter?"

Our earnest, well-intended effort to create an informed community and get everyone on a level playing field had failed utterly. The muttered asides, evidently by individuals who figured they could read between the lines to get at what must be the real, hidden agendas of those government experts at the head table, had been the only information effectively transmitted at either meeting. The Mountain View meeting, in particular, took place against a backdrop of rumour and conspiracy theories from friends and relatives in Idaho and Utah. Down there, at that same time, a hot debate was playing out over the impending introduction of Canadian wolves to Yellowstone National Park and central Idaho's big wilderness areas.

We had thought the meetings had delivered a fairly simple message: "Those wolves you've been seeing? We're hoping to radio-collar a few. If you shoot any, please pick ones without collars first so we can learn as much as possible from the collared ones. And we'll let everyone know what we learn."

Apparently the message actually communicated, in spite of it being somewhere the other side of the Twilight Zone in terms of reality, was that American biologists would shortly be releasing fifty protected wolves near Payne Lake, with Parks Canada's support, because of the US Endangered Species Act.

Nevertheless, a few weeks later, Joe arrived with Carter Niemeyer, a seasoned trapper who had spent many years with the US Animal Damage Control group but was now a wolf specialist with the US FWS. Although the American team would trap and collar the wolves, the ongoing monitoring responsibility was going to fall to Parks Canada and Alberta Fish and Wildlife. To that end, Richard and I had pooled our resources to hire a student assistant by the name of Elliot Fox. Elliot was a recent graduate of the Lethbridge Community College's renewable resources program, a deeply principled conservationist and passionately committed to helping make the Kainai (Blood) First Nation, of which he was a member, a leader in sustainable resource management and wildlife conservation.

The Belly wolves eluded Carter, Joe and Elliot. Fortunately, Diane Boyd had previously collared three young female wolves, including Salix, in the Montana Flathead that emigrated to Canada upon reaching maturity. Each became alpha female in a new pack. However unpleasant the collaring experience might be for a wolf, that impressive piece of neck adornment seems to enhance their subsequent social status. With Richard Quinlan's consent, since the other packs lived well north of the park, Elliot ended up monitoring all three packs.

The Belly pack denned in Waterton Lakes National Park and ranged south into Montana and north into the ranching landscape around Mountain View, occasionally crossing the Waterton River to the marginally friendlier west side. The Beauvais pack denned on private land southwest of Pincher Creek, ranging through ranch country and up into the provincial public lands along the Rocky Mountain Front. Their range overlapped with that of the Carbondale pack, which lived mostly on public lands in the upper Carbondale and Castle River drainages, as well as adjoining ranches.

Surprisingly, given the abundance of cattle in that corner of Alberta, the wolves fitted in well. The Belly River wolves, for example, hunted white-tailed deer, elk and beaver in forested grazing areas full of domestic cattle – without once succumbing to the temptation to eat beef. By now I knew several ranchers whose land the wolves hunted adjacent to the national park. Although all were sure it was just a matter of time before the immigrant wolves would begin to wreak havoc with their herds, none could find any evidence of wolves chasing cattle. The Beauvais wolves, in fact, denned in a cow pasture. Local residents reported seeing them hunting ground squirrels near cows and once chasing a deer right through a herd of cattle. The cows stared, and then went back to grazing.

The manager of that ranch, come fall hunting season, actually told visiting hunters that they could shoot deer and elk on his ranch but must leave the wolves strictly alone. He didn't want his well-behaved pack replaced by others with a less benign attitude toward cows.

Other wolves north of the area, however, discovered a taste for Alberta beef and were soon confirming the dire predictions of naysayers. West of Highway 22, in the Whaleback and Breeding Valley areas, one elusive and seldom-seen pack became particularly notorious, killing or wounding cattle on a regular basis over a period of several months. In some cases, the wolves killed and fed on their prey. Sometimes they left their victims badly wounded from unsuccessful attacks.

In spite of concerted efforts by problem-wildlife staff of Alberta Fish and Wildlife to find and kill them, by the spring of 1995 the wolves had killed or painfully mauled at least thirty cows.

No Free Lunch

After the Twin Butte and Mountain View meetings, we needed to address the misinformation and distrust. Clearly, more meetings would not solve that problem. Elliot and I began, instead, to find opportunities simply to visit the neighbours at their homes. Elliot had another reason, as he needed permission to access property in his ongoing efforts to locate the radio signals of the highly mobile wolves. Richard, too, because of his various responsibilities as a wildlife manager in southwestern Alberta, was soon knocking on ranch house doors and drinking coffee at kitchen tables.

It was the right way to communicate with rural people. Wolf research, on the other hand, was not always the most productive topic to open with. Even so, most of the people I met were decent, deep-thinking individuals who took quiet pride in their stewardship of the land. Their feelings about wolves were often not so much hostile as troubled. The annual calf crop provided their family incomes. They couldn't be out there day in and day out keeping an eye on things. They didn't trust experts to get anything right. They might be inclined simply to ignore wolves, but they couldn't: the stakes were too great.

It didn't help any that, by the 1990s, Alberta's progressive era under Peter Lougheed was over. A much more reactionary government under Ralph Klein was busy undoing much of what the Lougheed Tories had accomplished. Klein, unfortunately, was a one-idea premier. His one idea was to cut spending. First he cut spending to eliminate deficit budgets. Then, rather than start investing in a positive vision for the province, he kept right on cutting, this time to eliminate the province's debt. He de-funded just about everything, even Alberta's once-impressive Heritage Trust Fund.

Finally, running out of reasons to cut, he started sending oil royalty rebate cheques to Albertans.

One of the victims of the Klein government's cost-cutting obsession was a long-standing program that had paid compensation to farmers and ranchers who lost livestock to predator kills. It was not an expensive program. According to the 1991 Wolf Management Plan for Alberta, total payouts averaged less than $50,000 per year, province-wide.

Although cutting the compensation program had virtually no impact on the province's debt, it sent shock waves through wolf country. Ranchers and farmers felt abandoned just as predator populations were increasing. With no prospect of compensation, they stopped calling Fish and Wildlife, further isolating themselves with their fears while also leaving Fish and Wildlife deaf and blind about what might or might not be happening in wolf country.

It soon became clear that compensation for livestock losses could make or break wolf management in southwestern Alberta. Some ranchers simply felt that wolves had no place in cattle country ever, under any circumstances. But others said they could continue to live with the risk of bear, coyote, cougar and occasional wolf predation as they always had, but not if the reward for their tolerance was lost income.

Appropriately humbled, now that we had a whole different problem to solve than the one we had started working on, we put our heads together to find a solution. There seemed little hope of persuading the provincial government to change its mind; some of the other sectors being burned by Klein-era budget cuts were a lot more influential than ranchers. The government was unlikely to risk a precedent by restoring compensation funding.

Any funds would have to come from those with the strongest stake in seeing wolves in southwestern Alberta. Certainly Waterton Lakes National Park's thousands of visitors, for the most part, wanted to see healthy natural ecosystems with the full range of native species, especially iconic large predators like grizzlies and wolves. Members of major environmental organizations, too, had a passion for wild nature. There were a lot of people who valued wolves; just not the ones on whose lands those wolves spent most of their time.

Defenders of Wildlife, south of the US border,

had been compensating ranchers for wolf and grizzly kills for several years already – only fair, since those predators were fully protected under the US Endangered Species Act. Although Alberta wolves weren't protected, we decided to try something similar. We felt strongly that those whose good stewardship of southwestern Alberta's natural landscapes exposed them to risks from predators should be able to recoup any losses. It might also help to build bridges between two groups who, up till then, mostly talked about each other, not to each other.

The Waterton Natural History Association, a volunteer-based organization that helps Parks Canada educate park visitors, agreed to solicit donations from park visitors on condition that their funds go to compensate local ranchers suffering losses due to "park" wolves. It was a good start, but the program had to cover a larger area and Richard felt we needed to cover losses from grizzly bears too.

In the early 1990s, most mainstream environmental groups had not yet come to terms with the important role that ranching plays in keeping natural landscapes intact. Cattle were largely seen as bad news. When the Canadian Parks and Wilderness Society also stepped up to the plate, it was an unprecedented and enlightened act of risk-taking. Mike Going, then the president of the Calgary chapter of CPAWS, was the visionary who persuaded his group to solicit donations from its membership to compensate any livestock losses to grizzlies or wolves south of the Highwood River, not just in the Waterton area.

The one thing we could not offer the funders was increased protection for wolves in southern Alberta. The compensation program would be strictly a goodwill initiative aimed at building social tolerance and reducing the risk of organized, unofficial eradication campaigns. The only slight improvement in survival prospects for wolves might come from discussions between ranchers and Fish and Wildlife officers, since our new, locally grown compensation program would again require confirmation of any kills. Those field conversations could lead to problem-solving ideas to reduce the risk of future predation losses – and, consequently, the urge for future retaliatory wolf killing.

Even without any new measures to keep wolves

alive, the bank account for the new Southwestern Alberta Wolf/Grizzly Livestock Compensation Program began, slowly, to fill. The steering committee included Richard Quinlan, representing Alberta Fish and Wildlife; myself for Parks Canada; Mike Going for the environmental community; and a Beaver Mines area rancher by the name of Keith Everts, representing the Alberta Cattle Commission. Rick Neville, a sheep rancher, rounded the group out.

Mike had grown up on a ranch near Longview. Now, when not representing CPAWS, he ran Good Earth Cafés in Calgary, a growing chain that catered primarily to vegetarian and vegan clients. The ponytailed and upbeat Keith was a former hippy and vegetarian who with his wife, Bev, had gotten into ranching through a farm apprenticeship program they signed up for in the 1970s. He and several other ranchers were building their Diamond Willow brand of organic and sustainably produced beef. So we had a former rancher who now ran vegetarian restaurants, and a former vegetarian who now ran a beef ranch. The Alberta Cattle Commission may have been a bit skeptical about the mix, so Keith was soon joined by the late

Kim Hansen, a multi-generation rancher from just outside Waterton Lakes National Park. Kim had no enthusiasm for wolves, but he understood the cattle business.

The steering committee decided to offer full fall-market-value compensation for confirmed kills, considerably better than the former government program. We suspected it wouldn't take long for the first claim to come in, since wolves were killing and maiming yearling cattle west of Highway 22 in the northern part of our area. But paranoia and conspiracy theories out on the range were evidently stronger than the hopeful idealism and out-of-the-box thinking that characterized our steering committee meetings. Word soon came back that influential skeptics were lobbying those who lost cows not to apply for compensation because the money was coming from environmentalists. They insisted that there were bound to be strings attached. Next thing, the naysayers darkly predicted, environmentalists would start telling them how to run their ranches.

Our frustration came to a head in early 1995, when a rancher from north of Pincher Creek finally contacted Fish and Wildlife and said he would like to be compensated for the loss of a yearling cow. Fish and Wildlife confirmed that it was a wolf kill. Since CPAWS was managing the funds, Mike Going arranged to send a cheque for $1,000 to the rancher. A few days later, he called to tell me that the cheque had been returned. Paranoid neighbours had persuaded the rancher that if he cashed an "environmental" cheque, it would be the thin edge of the wedge leading to total protection for wolves. Distrust triumphed over bridge-building.

Behind the scenes, meanwhile, the Alberta Cattle Commission had been lobbying the Alberta government about their fears that environmental groups were getting too involved in predator management. They also stressed the unfairness of having compensation available only to south-western livestock producers when other parts of the province had losses too. Unlikely though it might have seemed a few months earlier, the Klein government quietly reinstated their province-wide taxpayer-funded livestock compensation program. Our effort to build bridges of respect and collaboration among the various sectors of society touched by the presence of wolves ended just as quietly.

The wolves were mostly dead by then anyway.

Wolves and Beef

Francis and Bonnie Gardner ranch in a spectacular landscape west of Highway 22 – Alberta's "Cowboy Trail." Lying just north of the Whaleback, their Mount Sentinel Ranch sits in the middle of some of the best deer and elk country in Alberta, and in a valley that serves as a travel corridor for wolves.

"I've lost all kinds of stock to wolves over the years," said Francis when I interviewed him in the late 1990s for a magazine article.

Wind-burned and thoughtful, Francis Gardner is like many second- and third-generation Alberta ranchers. He takes pride in the health of his land and the abundant wildlife it supports. He described his ranch to me as a "working wilderness." Normally, he was philosophical about the fact that his good management made it inevitable that wolves would turn up sooner or later. When wolves killed his livestock, however, Mr. Gardner's live-and-let-live philosophy had to give way to hard-nosed pragmatism. He couldn't afford to lose those cows.

> I only recall two cases where I had to take action about wolves. The worst one was when a pack of wolves killed eight head over two weeks in 1994. One time I could hear the commotion in the night – cows bawling and coyotes in the distance making all kinds of weird noises. That time I called Fish and Wildlife and they put in a strychnine bait station and killed three wolves. The other time was in early 1995. We lost two yearling heifers a week apart. There was only one wolf that time. My son was sleeping with the window partly open and heard the panicked bawling of the cow around 2 a.m.

The Belly, Beauvais and Carbondale packs, having been founded by well-protected and over-monitored wolves from Montana, included radio-collared animals that biologists could monitor. The Whaleback wolves – likely a pack originating from Canada, where wolves have never had an effective Endangered Species Act to lull them into complacency – unfortunately did not. Without radio collars, Alberta's Fish and Wildlife officers had to rely on chance in their efforts to track the problem wolves. They tried hard to live-trap the wolves, but eventually had to set out poison bait stations when their efforts to radio-collar wolves failed and the cattle depredations continued.

By the time the Gardners lost their last heifer in early 1995, almost all the wolves in southwestern Alberta had already died at the hands of humans. Trappers killed fifteen. A truck killed one on a highway west of Pincher Creek. Hunters shot several during the fall hunting season. Individual ranchers shot a few too. Ironically, the cattle-killing wolves west of the Cowboy Trail were among the last to die. Wildlife officers poisoned four and shot one.

The Belly, Beauvais and Carbondale packs were among the first to go. Open country and abundant roads between Pincher Creek and Waterton Lakes National Park had made it impossible for the wolves to stay out of sight for long. That, combined with Alberta's liberal policies around the killing of wolves, guaranteed their doom.

Not that their doom bothered many ranchers.

"Our grandparents went to a lot of trouble to get rid of wolves," one Mountain View area rancher had said to me after our 1994 meeting. "Why would we want to let them come back now?" It was common knowledge that some of his neighbours had been setting illegal poison baits out for bears and wolves, but the poachers were never caught.

The prevailing sentiment that wolves and ranching don't mix has deep roots. When settlers first brought cattle to stock western ranges a century ago, bison were newly extinct, elk had virtually disappeared and deer were rare. But wolves still persisted and they needed food. Early ranchers left their cattle and horses free to range over vast areas. The desperate wolves soon learned to kill them.

Today, however, wolf food is abundant. Elk, deer and other wild prey are so common that Alberta and other provinces are unable to sell all the available hunting licences. In parts of southern Alberta, where deer hunting was prohibited until the late 1950s, hunters who apply for a doe mule deer licence sometimes receive two tags instead of one.

Ranching is different now, too, than it was two

generations ago. Most cows now give birth to their calves in fenced pastures near their owners' homes rather than out on the open range. Ranchers closely tend their herds much of the year. Some clean up the carcasses of cows and sheep that die of natural causes, rather than leaving them out where wolves or bears that scavenge the remains might develop an interest in nearby herds. Others use livestock guard dogs or, where they summer their cattle on remote grazing licences in the Forest Reserve, employ range riders to keep an eye on things and discourage predators.

Half a century of wolf research has yielded new understanding of wolves too. John Gunson, long-time Alberta provincial carnivore specialist, studied two wolf packs west of Rocky Mountain House in the 1970s. He found that one pack killed mostly elk while the other killed mostly moose, even though both ranged through the same area. Wolves, it turns out, are not random killers. Like dogs, wolves learn through experience to do things most likely to yield a reward. Consequently, most wolf packs develop hunting patterns that select for specific kinds of prey. They don't bother with other potential prey, because they don't have experience hunting it and they already know how and where to get their next meal.

Shot on Suspicion

Why did the Belly River and Beauvais wolf packs choose not to kill the numerous cows and calves they encountered during the course of their daily hunts? It's a question that researchers never got the chance to answer. Based on earlier research by Gunson and others, however, they probably simply did not recognize cows as potential prey. They were looking for what they had hunted successfully before: deer and elk.

On the other hand, why did the Gardners and their neighbours, a hundred kilometres farther north, lose so many cows to wolves? Perhaps their wolves were strangers who did not yet know how to hunt that particular landscape. Or they simply had learned how to hunt and kill yearling cattle and gotten good at it. No one will ever know now; wolves just don't last long enough in foothills ranching country to make it worth the expense of studying them.

Clearly, however, karma played no role. The Belly wolves spared the cattle of dyed-in-the-wool wolf-haters, while the Whaleback pack preyed on the herds of some ranchers who were otherwise prepared to live and let live.

A study of wolf–livestock interactions in BC concluded that "although possibly all wolves can kill livestock, not all do. Since wolves patrol their own territories more intensively and effectively than a predator control officer is likely to be able to, possibly the best line of defence against wolves which may kill livestock is an established pack which doesn't. That is, removal of such a pack may do more harm than good."

The wolves that Katie and I watched in 1996 were a new pack filling the vacuum left by the unfortunate slaughter of the Belly pack over the preceding months. Later that winter, our whole family spotted them again. Each lay on its own separate knoll in the rolling fescue grasslands at the north end of Waterton Lakes National Park, near a wintering elk herd. The large black male stared back, unperturbed, as we studied them through the telescope. We left with the feeling these latest wild hunters had found their way home.

Then, that April, history repeated itself. A

rancher and a hunting guide shot two wolves in an open meadow adjacent to the Birdseye Ranch's calving pasture, just outside the park. One was the large black male. The other, a smaller grey, was a pregnant female carrying six unborn pups.

The rancher told me that when they opened the wolves' bellies, he was surprised to find only the remains of deer. For all his dislike of wolves, I could tell he was rethinking his assumptions about them. But for the wolves it was too late. Once again, preconceived notions and lax regulations had destroyed a southwestern Alberta wolf pack. Just like the earlier Belly wolves, the new pack had never been known to kill a cow. It didn't matter. They were shot just in case.

Some of those who killed the wolves may have thought they were heading off future problems; instead they created a public relations problem for their fellow ranchers. Public outrage over all the unwarranted wolf killings in the mid-1990s led many environmentalists to dust off old complaints about how ranchers control too much land and seem to care too little about other people's values.

Unlike the ranchers who killed the wolves near Waterton, Bonnie Gardner knows what it's like to lose valuable livestock to wild predators. But neither she nor her husband supports the idea of killing a wolf just because it's there. "We have to make room for nature," she told me. "It's too easy to try and solve your troubles by just killing things. But if you take that far enough, you just end up sterilizing the landscape. No one can live in a sterile landscape."

Francis agreed. "Wolves are an important part of the whole system. We need them out there."

The Gardners received the World Wildlife Fund's prestigious Alberta Prairie Conservation Award in 1995, only a few months after their latest livestock loss to wolves. The award recognized the couple's long commitment to preserving prairie grassland – among Canada's most endangered ecosystems – and their efforts to protect native biodiversity on a working cattle ranch.

The Gardners market organic beef. They helped pioneer the use of fire to restore natural processes to foothills grasslands. They have repeatedly adjusted their grazing strategies to improve the ecological health of streams and riparian areas, using their ranch as a demonstration site to help educate others about sustainable range management.

Even so, when they need to – but only when they need to – they ask Alberta Fish and Wildlife to kill wolves on their ranch. The Gardners live in nature. They know that death and life are part of the same cycle. They are not repelled by the idea of killing a wolf to protect their livelihood, but neither are they repelled by the idea of wolves living, and killing other animals, on the land they care for.

What does repel them is the thought that public concern over wolves or other environmental issues could aggravate forces already threatening the survival of ranching in Alberta's chinook country.

The Importance of Ranching

Native bunchgrass prairie carpets the foothills slopes between the Mount Sentinel ranch and the nearby Rocky Mountains. Old-growth Douglas fir crowns the ridges; graceful thickets of aspen crowd the hollows and spill out onto willow-thick flats along Stimson Creek's beaver ponds and wetlands. Hundreds of mule deer and dozens of elk graze year round on the Gardners' hay meadows and native range. Cougars hunt the forest edges. From time to time, wolves pull down an elk or deer.

On any satellite photograph of western Canada, the landscape shows the marks of a century of rapid change. Little usable wolf habitat survives amid the checker-squares of wheat fields, polka-dot patterns of irrigation fields, and mange-like sprawl of growing cities and towns. A narrow band of foothills country along the eastern flanks of the Rocky Mountains, however, remains relatively intact. Some of the best remaining wildlife habitat left outside of the national parks, it survived the twentieth century's hasty changes solely because it remained under the control of ranchers like the Gardners.

Those windblown, game-rich Alberta foothills are prime wolf habitat. And with wolves protected to the south by the prospect of re-listing under the US Endangered Species Act and to the west by national parks and BC's responsible hunting regulations, wolves will continue to disperse into that habitat.

The only way to get rid of wolves now would be to eliminate their habitat. And that could happen.

Each time oil or gas prices peak, boom times return to Alberta. With each burst of wealth, new subdivisions appear in the foothills. Roads and monster homes continue to sprawl out from major highways and towns into the heart of ranching country – not only in southwestern Alberta but in southern BC and northern Montana too. As recreational acreages proliferate, land prices and taxes climb. Ranchers can find themselves squeezed by low cattle prices and high land costs. Selling out to real estate speculators begins to look more reasonable every year, at least to some.

The Gardners are among a fortunate few who control not only their own deeded land but extensive grazing leases on public land too. Because ranchers want to control public access to those leases, hunters and environmentalists often become angry. It's public land, they say: why should a single rancher control our access to it? Compounding their frustration is the fact that lease rates on public lands are relatively low and licences to graze Forest Reserve lands even cheaper.

On the other hand, those large tracts of public land, interspersed with private fields, are generally ecologically healthy because of careful and caring stewardship. Most of the lousy ranchers went out of business (or into real estate development) long ago. It's no accident that wolves want to live there.

A certain amount of public subsidy in the form of low lease rates ensures long-term protection of open spaces and wildlife habitat.

"I read somewhere that 80 per cent of Canada's population used to be agricultural," Francis Gardner told me back in 1996. "Over the past sixty years, this has dropped to only around 2.5 per cent. Now most of the country's wealth comes from non-renewable resources and urban areas. We don't seem to see the land, and people on the land, as an important resource so much anymore."

The people on the land today are the ones whose care and stewardship have made southwestern Alberta prime wolf habitat. Many, admittedly, don't want wolves there. But the wolves will keep coming back, because ranching helps ensure that game is abundant and people scarce in the foothills. Alberta's primitive wolf regulations may make it difficult to manage wolves sensibly, but that doesn't change the fact that wolves keep finding their way home.

Most ranchers are thinking people; that's what ensures their survival in a challenging occupation. Each time wolves find their way home, even if they survive for only a few months, foothills ranchers get another chance to know real wolves, rather than mythical ones. Knowledge and understanding arising from personal experience are sure antidotes to prejudice and fear.

Ranchers who know and live with wolves may well hold the key to the future – both for public land ranching and for Alberta's foothills wolves.

That's the irony of the perceived conflict between wolves and livestock. The future survival of southwestern Alberta's wolves may well depend on the future survival of the family ranch. And the survival of the family ranch, in a world where wolves seem to have more friends than do ranchers, may depend no less strongly on the willingness of ranchers to live with a challenging, potentially costly, predator. That tolerance can only develop if ranchers have a chance to live with wolves and get to understand them for what they really are, rather than the ravening cattle killers that myths and rumours make them out to be.

Francis Gardner suggested a fairly simple set of guidelines for managing wolves in cattle country: "Give the wildlife officers authority to control the wolves that do the killing. Protect the ones that don't. If you can compensate for the killings, then a lot of ranchers won't be so touchy. And it would help if you could let ranchers know how wolves fit into the scheme of things, educate them about wolves, so they can make their own decisions. The big mistake is the people and groups who try to impose solutions on ranchers." I asked wolf biologists Carolyn Callaghan and Paul Paquet their thoughts: they agreed.

Unfortunately, Alberta's antiquated regulations guarantee continued failure. Virtually anyone can kill as many wolves as they want in Alberta, regardless of whether those wolves hunt cattle or live on wild game. Alberta regulations provide that a landowner may shoot a wolf at any time on or within eight kilometres of his or her land; any other Albertan, on land to which he or she has right of access, may shoot a wolf during approximately nine months of each year (September through May); and trappers may kill as many wolves as they wish.

For wolves, unlike other animals, the pack rather than the individual is the functional social unit. Random killing of individual wolves, which is what current wildlife regulations promote, is a recipe for continuing conflict. It disrupts functional packs and can trigger changes in hunting behaviour. It may also have the perverse effect of freeing subordinate pack members to breed, resulting in higher pup production than if the alpha animals were kept alive: more wolves, and more unpredictable wolves.

It doesn't help that third parties sometimes arrogate the management of wolves to themselves rather than leaving wildlife management to the responsible agencies. As recently as 2012, hunting clubs like the Sundre Fish and Game Association and municipal governments like the county of Cardston were paying out bounties on dead wolves. Their efforts not only guaranteed unintended consequences and chaotic results but also cut Fish and Wildlife – the agency responsible for managing wildlife in the whole public interest – right out of the picture. No less wrong-headed is the behind-the-scenes connivance between some hunting outfitters and fur trappers who count wolves from private helicopters and then decide how many will die in order to maximize profits for the outfitters.

Enlightened wolf management is possible. But it certainly won't happen if special interest groups or rural municipal governments continue to be permitted to override provincial wildlife policies with freelance programs that kill wolves indiscriminately. Random, untargeted wolf killing is not responsible management – it is simply an assertion of stubborn prejudice, as self-defeating as it is mindless.

Government agencies need to reassert their primary authority to manage wolves. Regulations that protect wolf packs not known to kill domestic livestock would be a good start.

Environmentalists, however, will also need to change. Treating each dead wolf as an outrage and a disaster is no less mindless than the actions of those who want all wolves dead. Instead, for the benefit of the overall wolf population, packs that prey on cattle have to go.

Wolves are neither evil nor sacred; they are wolves. We need to manage them based on their biology, not our attitudes and biases. That applies on both the anti-wolf and the pro-wolf side of the equation. As one biologist said to me after the frustrating outcome of events of the 1990s in southwestern Alberta, "It would sure help if everyone stopped doing everything back-asswards."

The Next, Best Place

Montana bills itself as "the last, best place," based on the title of a book by William Kittredge and Annick Smith. What a great slogan. No surprise that advocacy groups have often borrowed it for wilderness protection campaigns.

When it's put to work in the service of conservation, however, the phrase carries an element of hopelessness. It aligns with the underlying defeatism of a twentieth-century environmentalism that was premised on the notion of inevitable loss. Wilderness campaigns often derived their urgency from the sense that, as Kurt Vonnegut once wrote: "Everything is going to get worse and worse and never get better again." Too many of those conservation campaigns were rooted in the desperate notion that, since North American progress must inevitably be at the expense of wild places and wild things, the best we could hope would be to try and hang on to the last good bits.

Late in the twentieth century, some of the movement's leading visionaries and thinkers grew impatient with man-the-lifeboats rhetoric and "last chance" campaigns. For one thing, a jaded public was becoming less and less responsive to Chicken Little's alarums. The world was going to end unless we protected Clayoquot Sound. Then the world was going to end unless we saved Haida Gwaii. That campaign concluded; next the world was going to end unless we kept loggers out of the Great Bear Rainforest.

The world didn't end. But even though those campaigns yielded some successes, the world didn't get much better either.

In truth, it was becoming increasingly clear to thinking conservationists that, while the biologically diverse and ecologically healthy world we had always taken for granted might not end, it was becoming a much poorer place in spite of the protection for some of its best surviving bits. Nature needed care not just in wilderness but everywhere. On a planet where, as John Muir once said, "When we try to pick out anything by itself, we find it hitched to everything else in the Universe," a few protected patches would never be enough to save biodiversity, healthy landscapes and natural processes.

In the early 1990s, I began hearing about a mapping project that framed a more activist conservation agenda. Drawing from the emerging sciences of conservation biology and landscape ecology, the Wildlands Project proposed a continent-wide system of protected core areas and connecting corridors of intact habitat, with carefully managed buffer areas surrounding both. Compelling as it seemed, it also sounded utterly unrealistic: clearly the product of academic intellectuals with little connection to the real world of politicians, lawyers and real estate speculators.

My reaction was predictable; I had grown up in a twentieth-century conservation movement that spoke only the language of staged retreats – not ambitious offensives.

With the Wildlands Project, activist David Foreman and conservation biologists Michael Soule and Reed Noss were among leading thinkers who challenged the rest of us to think beyond loss into hope; to consider the possibility of continental-scale nature restoration. Ironically, their hopeful vision for a renewed, ecologically whole North America arose in part from a seminal study by William Newmark, one of Soule's students, that was very much focused on loss.

Newmark reviewed the status of large mammal faunas in every national park in western North America. Up until then, prevalent social attitudes had seen conservation and protection as opposite from, and in opposition to, development and exploitation. Consequently, all those protected areas had been managed as islands of protection, surrounded by land that could and arguably should be used for more exploitative purposes.

Newmark's study, "A Land-Bridge Island Perspective on Mammalian Extinctions in Western North American Parks," published in the journal *Nature*, showed that the result of that approach was extinction: of all the large national parks that Canada and the United States had set aside in the preceding 120 years, only the Banff/Jasper/Yoho/Kootenay block of mountain national parks still had all the species it had started with. Every other protected area had already lost some of its original species, mostly because of changes to the surrounding landscape, where they had previously been able to range.

In fact, the Canadian mountain national parks had lost one species – plains bison – before they even became national parks. And only a decade after his paper's publication, Banff's last caribou perished. Jasper's caribou herds now appear to be plummeting toward oblivion too. Their fate simply reinforces Newmark's point. Parks are vital – but they're not enough.

Animals will go extinct anyway, in spite of park protection, if forced to persist only as small populations isolated from one another by increasingly nature-unfriendly landscapes.

Beyond a small core of activists, thinkers and ecologists, however, the Wildlands Project didn't get much traction. Most Canadians and Americans are philosophically sympathetic to, or even strongly support, the need to protect nature and natural places. But the population wasn't conditioned to the kind of ideas that the Wildlands Project challenged them to consider.

The Wildlands Project's board of directors at first included only one Canadian, Monte Hummel. In 1991 Monte co-authored a book with

Sherry Pettigrew entitled *Wild Hunters: Predators in Peril.* They were well ahead of their time in proposing a conservation strategy for Canada's large carnivore species, including wolves. The strategy called for large "Carnivore Conservation Areas" that included not only core protected areas but also much larger surrounding buffers where habitat, hunting and disturbance would be managed in ways that kept carnivores alive. It was as biologically sound, and politically unlikely, as the Wildlands Project.

Like the Wildlands Project, their vision was nonetheless part of a change in the language of conservation. It got Harvey Locke thinking. Harvey, then-president of the Canadian Parks and Wilderness Society, was another environmentalist who had grown impatient with rearguard actions founded on pessimism about what modern North American society is capable of achieving. At Monte's suggestion, the board of the Wildlands Project welcomed Harvey into the fold too.

Pluie and Opal

It was raining the day that biologist Paul Paquet found a five-year-old wolf waiting for him in a modified leg-hold trap he had set in Alberta's Peter Lougheed Provincial Park. That was 1991, the same year that Monte Hummel and Sherry Pettigrew published their ambitious conservation proposition for North America's wild hunters. Paul fitted the dripping wolf with a radio collar and quickly released her back into the wild. He named her Pluie, after the French word for rain.

If biologists had wanted to get a sense of how much terrain an individual wolf can traverse in its lifetime, they couldn't have chosen a better research subject. Over the next two years, the GPS tracking device embedded in waterproof resin in Pluie's new collar recorded an amazing story of long-distance travel.

Shortly after her release, Pluie moved north and became a member of Banff National Park's Cascade pack. It soon became apparent, however, that she didn't really consider herself an Alberta wolf. She was a citizen of a larger universe.

Within three years, Pluie had journeyed not once but twice through BC's Elk and Flathead valleys south into Montana, looped west in Idaho, then found her way back into the Alberta Rockies near Banff. On one of those trips, the satellites monitoring her radio signal indicated that she had trekked far to the east of Browning, Montana, into open prairie country.

Late in 1993, Pluie's bullet-damaged radio transmitter turned up on a mountainside near Fernie, BC. The rest of the collar, and the remains of Pluie herself, were missing. Paul assumed the wandering wolf had finally met her end. She hadn't. Two years later, a hunter near Invermere, BC, shot three wolves out of a pack that had established itself in nearby Kootenay National Park. One of the wolves was Pluie.

Pluie's travels had encompassed an area of more than one hundred thousand kilometres. She had crossed major Canadian highways and four-lane interstates, skirted countless towns, farms and mines, and left tracks along rivers draining to three oceans, in two Canadian provinces and three American states.

Opal, another wolf Paul Paquet radio-collared in the Kananaskis, travelled even farther south. Unlike Pluie, who had managed to stay out of trouble all her life, Opal fell prey to the temptation to sample Alberta beef. The rancher who caught her in the act in the Highwood River valley had his rifle handy. When he called Paul to tell him about the incident, he said that he was pretty sure he had hit her but hadn't been able to find the carcass.

That's because it wasn't there. Four years later, predator specialist Carter Niemeyer got a call to deal with a pack of wolves killing cattle just north of Yellowstone National Park. When Carter tracked down and killed the wolves, he found that the alpha female was none other than Opal. She had travelled well more than one thousand kilometres from her birth den. The journey took her the whole length of Montana – her last, best place.

Yellowstone to Yukon

For decades, hunting and conservation groups had waged isolated battles to save various parts of the western mountains from assaults by logging companies, gas exploration crews and coal miners, from overgrazing and from abuse by off-road-vehicle enthusiasts. Each campaign was in response to a specific new threat. Each involved mobilizing volunteers, capturing media attention and lobbying politicians all over again to save the latest "last, best place."

Harvey Locke helped lead many of those efforts, as well as fighting to protect existing protected areas, like Banff National Park, from new assaults by monied interests who saw opportunities to exploit wolf country for profit. The wildlife overpasses along the Trans-Canada Highway were, to a considerable degree, a product of his lobbying.

On a 1993 horse trip, Harvey found himself studying some maps while sitting beside a campfire in the northern BC's Muskwa-Kechika wilderness. The rolling tundra plateaux, hushed valleys and lush wildlife ranges that surrounded him were new country, yet strangely familiar to one well acquainted with the Rocky Mountain national parks farther south. He was reflecting on what Diane Boyd's and Paul Paquet's radio-collared study wolves were telling us about their need for big wild spaces. Too many of those spaces, however, had been left wounded by the twentieth century's surfeit of haste and ignorance. In an increasingly urbanized and distracted North American society, Harvey knew, restoring some wildness to the west could well prove no less vital for the physical, mental and spiritual well-being of humans than for wolves and other animals. But the challenge of motivating popular action for conservation continued to confound even those most passionate about the challenge. Far to the south of his party's lonely camp was Yellowstone – the world's first experiment with the idea of protecting nature in national parks. Beyond the dwarf birch meadows and rounded peaks to the north was the Yukon Territory, made famous in the poems of Robert Service. The Yukon remained a place with very few people and very large wilderness, where all the original animals and most of their habitat still survived, late in the twentieth century.

Yellowstone was the living embodiment of North America's ideal of protected nature. Yukon represented the living reality of vast, intact wilderness ecosystems. And between them was the Rocky Mountain cordillera – a landscape whose famous parks and wildlands have inspired and rewarded generations of North Americans who believe that grizzly bears, wolves, wildness and spectacular natural beauty will always help define us as Canadians or, south of the forty-ninth parallel, as Americans.

The only problem was, history was filling that middle bit with roads, towns, mines and clearcuts that made it increasingly difficult for those wide-ranging predators to travel from one part of the wilderness dream to another.

Harvey scribbled "Yellowstone to Yukon?" on the margin of one map, along with some ideas on conservation strategy for the region. It was the first record of a contagious idea that would finally change the conservation dialogue from pessimistic desperation to determined and aggressive optimism. He still has that map.

Six months later, Harvey and others from the Wildlands Project assembled several dozen biologists, conservation activists, hunters and hikers from across the continent at a small research station in Alberta's Kananaskis valley. Among those present were Paul Paquet, Monte Hummel, Reed Noss and others who had been inspired by the journeys of Pluie and Opal. By the time the two-day meeting had concluded, the Yellowstone to Yukon Conservation Initiative had been born. Hundreds gathered in Waterton Lakes National Park two years later for Yellowstone to Yukon's public launch.

Yellowstone to Yukon caught the public imagination immediately. The alliteration likely helped, but what was most powerful was the vision of linking the birthplace of the national park idea and the last truly vast wilderness landscapes surviving in North America at the end of the twentieth century. It became the spark that finally helped popularize the thinking behind the Wildlands Project.

Suddenly the conversation about nature conservation was no longer just based on what we could save, but on what we could give back to the wild things with whom we share our home places. Yellowstone to Yukon was about what we could recover and restore for the future – it was conservation based on inspired hope.

Some of America's earliest and best-loved Wilderness Areas lie north of Yellowstone – the Bob Marshall, Scapegoat, and Great Bear. Straddling the US-Canada border a little farther north is the world's first International Peace Park – comprised of Canada's Waterton Lakes and the US's Glacier National Park. Farther north yet, Canada's first national park – Banff – sits cheek-to-jowl with other great mountain parks: Kootenay, Yoho and Jasper National Parks and Mount Assiniboine, Peter Lougheed, Spray Valley, Hamber and Mount Robson Provincial Parks.

Lesser known but no less spectacular parks like Kakwa, Stone Mountain and Muncho Lake lie even farther north.

All have grizzlies, cougars, elk and other wilderness creatures. Since the US reintroductions to Yellowstone and Idaho, all have wolves now too. Yellowstone to Yukon proposes simply to ensure that that chain of protected areas trending north into the Yukon's big wild remains ecologically connected forever.

Wolves, grizzlies, wolverines and other wary animals live at low population densities. They have large home ranges and need to be able to disperse long distances. That makes them ideal indicators. If they can fully occupy the Yellowstone-to-Yukon region and continue to travel safely throughout it, then countless other species who also depend on landscape connectivity and healthy ecosystems should thrive too. And so, of course, will humans. In an increasingly crowded world, after all, we will need Wallace Stegner's "geography of hope" more than ever before.

The Yellowstone to Yukon geography of hope will likely have a few more parks and protected areas. Already, it helped create one of Canada's most remarkable conservation achievements of the last decade: the eight-fold expansion of the Nahanni National Park Reserve. Some other existing ones will need to be expanded too. Beyond their value as places of recreation, discovery and learning for thousands of world-weary visitors each year, they offer the highest degree of ecosystem protection and, as such, serve as insurance policies against conservation failure elsewhere. Parks are sanctuaries where wolves can raise their young in peace (nosy researchers and wildlife paparazzi notwithstanding) while avoiding bullets, traps and poison.

That geography will also, necessarily, contain logging, cattle ranching and oil and gas development. Notwithstanding our many twentieth-century mistakes, it is certainly possible to cut trees, graze cows and extract petroleum resources without seriously damaging ecosystems or displacing wildlife. It's possible; it's just too seldom done. Getting it right in the Yellowstone-to-Yukon region will challenge orthodoxy and cost both effort and money—but it will also create new possibilities for ecologically sustainable development elsewhere in the North American landscape. In a crowded future, we will need those possibilities.

Proof of the possible is no farther away than Banff National Park. When Parks Canada installed high fences and wildlife crossing structures along the Trans-Canada Highway, a twentieth-century road that had almost completely fragmented the Yellowstone-to-Yukon region became a model of landscape reconnection. There was a time when that was unimaginable. Now it's the new standard for highways in wildlife areas.

That same kind of innovative new thinking is possible in every resource domain. If Yellowstone to Yukon is to move from vision to reality, the once unthinkable needs to go from possibility to reality. In this century, it could.

In this century, frankly, it must.

Tracks on the Homeward Trail

It's aiming too low simply to save the last, best place, wherever that might be. It's just not enough: not for nature, and not for people. Nature and people, ultimately, are the same thing; we just have an unfortunate habit of forgetting that.

It's not the *last* but the *next*, best places that

will give us a future worth occupying. There are already tracks on the trails leading toward those next, best places. They are wolf tracks, interlaced with ours.

Some of those next, best places will have roads, but no more roads than absolutely necessary. Those roads will be designed so they don't kill wary predators or block them from moving freely through their home ranges. Some roads will lead to logging areas but not to the scarified clearcuts of twentieth-century forest exploitation. And where we have agreed to save some of the future for caribou, there will be neither roads nor logging – and we'll be okay with that, because we won't want to live in a place that could have saved its caribou and didn't. There will be wolf tracks there too, but not many. That's how it is in caribou country. Not all the next, best places will be the same.

In some, there will be elk and deer. They will be wild and watchful. They'll have to be. They will be healthy too; the unhealthy ones will have been eaten. With their genetic fitness and wary behaviour and their health constantly tended to by wolves, they will be the sort of elk and deer we humans find most rewarding to hunt and eat; a continuing gift of perfectedness from one North American predator to another.

Thriving stands of aspen will turn gold each fall; tall willows will droop over trout streams. Beavers will trace quiet lines across wetland ponds in the evening. Each spring day, the sun will rise to an explosion of birdsong – from tree-nesters, shrub-nesters and ground-nesters alike.

There will still be cattle in many of those next, best places. They will be as familiar with the smell of wolves as with the taste of rough fescue. Some wolf packs will learn to hunt those cattle. When wildlife officers kill those cattle-killers, environmental groups will not complain. And the ranchers will insist on leaving the other wolves alone.

Those next, best places will be our habitat too. We will feel wilder and more alive there than we may have once thought possible, because those wolf tracks will make us a little less certain of ourselves; a bit less in control. Humility tastes bitter only at first; then it starts to taste a lot like belonging. When we follow those tracks into the green landscapes they stitch together, we will find some fine things – both inside ourselves and outside.

The wolf, like the human, is a keystone species: one whose role in the ecosystem is so significant that its presence – or absence – changes everything. Wolves are already changing everything. If we are prepared to let them, they might even make us more human, because to share our home places with as formidable a predator and as canny a competitor as the wolf will challenge us to use all our finest human attributes: intelligence, adaptability, innovation, humility and compassion. Too often, our historical determination to live without the wolf brought out our worst – ignorance, fear, intolerance and cruelty.

Even were we to strive to perpetuate the errors of the past, opting for those worst attributes, we would soon find that we don't have that option anyway. There are wolf tracks on too many of the homeward trails, pointing their way toward those next, best places that could define our tomorrow. Some wolves are already here; others will follow.

Those homeward wolves were likely sent not so much to test us as to teach us. They will keep on returning until we finish learning how to live with them. Then we, like the wolf, will at last have arrived home in the next, great places we were always meant to share.

Bookshelf

Alberta Fish and Wildlife Division. *Management Plan for Wolves in Alberta*. Wildlife Management Planning Series, no. 4. Edmonton: Alberta Forestry, Lands & Wildlife, December 1991. Accessed (pdf) May 15, 2013, http://is.gd/gMwrNX.

Eisenberg, Cristina. *The Wolf's Tooth: Keystone Predators, Trophic Cascades and Biodiversity*. Washington, DC: Island Press, 2010.

Gunson, John R. *Historical and Present Management of Wolves in Alberta*. Wildlife Society Bulletin 20, no. 3 (Autumn 1992): 330–339.

Hummel, Monte, Sherry Pettigrew and Robert Bateman. *Wild Hunters: Predators in Peril*. Toronto: Key Porter, 1991.

Leopold, Aldo. *A Sand County Almanac with Essays on Conservation from Round River*. New York: Ballantine Books, 1986.

McNamee, Thomas. *The Return of the Wolf to Yellowstone*. New York: Henry Holt Owl Books, 1998.

Mech, L. David, and Luigi Boitani, eds. *Wolves: Behavior, Ecology and Conservation*. Chicago: University of Chicago Press, 2007.

Meredith, Don H., and Duane Radford, eds. *Conservation, Pride and Passion: The Alberta Fish and Game Association, 1908–2008*. Edmonton: Alberta Fish and Game Association, 2008.

Niemeyer, Carter. *Wolfer: A Memoir*. Boise, Idaho: Bottlefly Press, 2010.

Rowledge, Darrel. *No Accident ... Public Policy and Chronic Wasting Disease in Canada*. Edmonton: Alberta Professional Outfitters Society, 2008.

Van Tighem, Kevin. *Predators: Wild Dogs and Cats*. Canmore, Alta.: Altitude, 1999.

Other Titles in this Series

The Earth Manifesto

Saving Nature
with Engaged
Ecology

David Tracey

ISBN 978-1-927330-89-0

Saving Lake Winnipeg

Robert William
Sandford

ISBN 978-1-927330-86-9

On Fracking

C. Alexia Lane

ISBN 978-1-927330-80-7

Little Black Lies

Corporate and
Political Spin
in the Global War
for Oil

Jeff Gailus

ISBN 978-1-926855-68-4

Digging the City

An Urban
Agriculture
Manifesto

Rhona McAdam

ISBN 978-1-927330-21-0

Gift Ecology

Reimagining a
Sustainable World

Peter Denton

ISBN 978-1-927330-40-1

The Insatiable Bark Beetle

Dr. Reese Halter

ISBN 978-1-926855-67-7

The Incomparable Honeybee

and the Economics
of Pollination
Revised & Updated

Dr. Reese Halter

ISBN 978-1-926855-65-3

The Beaver Manifesto

Glynnis Hood

ISBN 978-1-926855-58-5

The Grizzly Manifesto

In Defence of the
Great Bear

Jeff Gailus

ISBN 978-1-897522-83-7

Becoming Water

Glaciers in a
Warming World

Mike Demuth

ISBN 978-1-926855-72-1

Ethical Water

Learning To Value
What Matters
Most

Robert William
Sandford
& Merrell-Ann S.
Phare

ISBN 978-1-926855-70-7

Denying the Source

The Crisis of First
Nations Water
Rights

Merrell-Ann S.
Phare .

ISBN 978-1-897522-61-5

The Weekender Effect

Hyperdevelopment
in Mountain
Towns

Robert William
Sandford

ISBN 978-1-897522-10-3

RMB saved the following resources by printing the pages of this book on chlorine-free paper made with 100% post-consumer waste:

Trees · 7, fully grown
Water · 3,366 gallons
Energy · 3 million BTUs
Solid Waste · 226 pounds
Greenhouse Gases · 620 pounds

CALCULATIONS BASED ON RESEARCH BY ENVIRONMENTAL DEFENSE AND THE PAPER TASK FORCE. MANUFACTURED AT FRIESENS CORPORATION.